Hoodoo

The Complete Guide to Working Conjure

(Working Magic Spells in Rootwork and Conjure With Roots)

Charles Reeves

Published By **Simon Dough**

Charles Reeves

All Rights Reserved

Hoodoo: The Complete Guide to Working Conjure (Working Magic Spells in Rootwork and Conjure With Roots)

ISBN 978-1-7774403-8-1

No part of this guidebook shall be reproduced in any form without permission in writing from the publisher except in the case of brief quotations embodied in critical articles or reviews.

Legal & Disclaimer

The information contained in this book is not designed to replace or take the place of any form of medicine or professional medical advice. The information in this book has been provided for educational & entertainment purposes only.

The information contained in this book has been compiled from sources deemed reliable, and it is accurate to the best of the Author's knowledge; however, the Author cannot guarantee its accuracy and validity and cannot be held liable for any errors or omissions. Changes are periodically made to this book. You must consult your doctor or get professional medical advice before using any of the suggested remedies, techniques, or information in this book.

Upon using the information contained in this book, you agree to hold harmless the Author from and against any damages, costs, and expenses, including any legal fees potentially resulting from the application of any of the information provided by this guide. This disclaimer applies to any damages or injury caused by the use and application, whether directly or indirectly, of any advice or information presented, whether for breach of contract, tort, negligence, personal injury, criminal intent, or under any other cause of action.

You agree to accept all risks of using the information presented inside this book. You need to consult a professional medical practitioner in order to ensure you are both able and healthy enough to participate in this program.

Table Of Contents

Chapter 1: Hoodoo Beliefs 1

Chapter 2: Hoodoo Ingredients And Materials... 13

Chapter 3: Hoodoo Spiritual Cleansing... 27

Chapter 4: Hoodoo Mojo Bag................. 39

Chapter 5: Conjure Work 47

Chapter 6: The Use Of Candle Magic...... 64

Chapter 7: Rootwork............................... 78

Chapter 8: Hoodoo Divination 90

Chapter 9: Hoodoo Spells For Love And Luck 105

Chapter 10: A Background On Hoodoo 119

Chapter 11: The Foundations Of Hoodoo 131

Chapter 12: Candle Magic..................... 153

Chapter 13: Mojo Bags.......................... 167

Chapter 14: Hoodoo Prayers................. 180

Chapter 15: Breaking Hexes 183

Chapter 1: Hoodoo Beliefs

Hoodoo is a wide selection of religious beliefs, allowing its adherents to take on the teachings of other religions. Hoodoo does not have to adhere to a particular set of rules and the practitioners can decide which type of Hoodooism is best for them.

The core convictions of Hoodoo can be easily recognized in the present day. The beliefs of Hoodoo give practitioners the foundation of their beliefs instead of limiting the practice. Practitioners are free to pick the gods they prefer to follow. They they aren't judged or criticized regardless of whom they decide to consult.

Hoodoo Core Beliefs

Divine Providence

First thing that comes to your mind when "Divine Providence" mentions it is God. The reason is that conventional theism is based on one primary figure, who has the control over the universe. This belief system teaches the belief that there exists a god who is the sole the sole source of all things. Hoodoo does not demand that people follow a single god, and only one god.

In Hoodoo It's not uncommon for people to include several gods within their religion so long as they satisfy their requirements. As an example, they could invoke Jesus for protection or healing as well as appeal to Santa Muertos to help them locate a suitable partner.

Death

For the rootworkers, dying isn't necessarily the end of the road. It is actually the practice of many to invoke their ancestral paternal ancestors for guidance in their lives. The practitioners of Hoodoo believe that once the body dies and the soul rises up to an higher level to be an ancestral figure. The living relatives are able to ask them for advice when they require it. The ancestral relatives also seek to intercede in spiritual higher powers on behalf of living relatives.

Clairvoyance

One of the most potent tools available to a doctor of conjuration is sight. People who can discern the future, and also communicate with spirits are given a better reputation in the society. Through this ability, they have the ability to move freely between future and past to determine the right solution to the current issue. Divination lets them participate in the lives of others in order to turn their lives to the right direction.

The Doctrine of Signatures

Hoodoo follows the concept of the signature, teaching that plants have characteristics that are indicative of diseases they are able to be able to treat or treat. Hoodoo claims that there's the cosmic signature of each and every thing in the universe that signifies its function or the intended usage.

Walnuts, for example, appear like our brains. In the past, healers believed that these nuts proved effective in treating diseases that were related to the brain. Now, we know that they are high in fatty acids which can assist in improving memory.

Stinging nettles, on other hand, possess hairs similar to that of the human head. Traditional healers utilize the nettles as lotion or cream to improve blood circulation and, can in turn help grow hair for people who are bald. In the same time hairs appear like stings of animals, making it a great treatment to combat insect bites and stings.

There's also lungwort, which is a plant that has black spots that look like the ones you see of a lung that is infected. Because of this, the plant is utilized to treat lung ailments including tuberculosis asthma and coughs.

Retributive Justice

Hoodoo is primarily practiced for helping improve the lives of humans. Many religions and philosophy promote that it is important to treat others with respect and not causing hurt to anyone else. For Hoodoo but, it's the idea of being an "eye for eye" that was derived direct from Bible. Hoodoo believes that all people have the right to seek justice. That's why Hoodoo lets its followers apply retributive justice in ways that inflict damage to oppressors by inflicting injury or any other type of hurt.

Intention

A few Hoodoo beliefs suggest that there is a mystical power to curses on other people. The practitioners believe that these curses, hexes and jinxes only function if the individual they're aimed at deserves to be cursed. They usually use powders that have intentions. In this case, for example, you can get"The Boss Fix," which is a powder that's designed to Boss Fix, a powder that is designed to convince your boss into putting them back in the same position.

Also, there's the Confusion Powder which is intended to mislead people who are at you from a bad motive. It's the Court Case Powder, on the other hand, can be employed to influence judges as well as the jury at courtroom. The Hotfoot Sachets serve to disengage people from your existence, while The Devil's Shoestring Sachet is used to keep enemies in check.

They also can only be effective if those whom they're aimed at truly merit the it. Boss Fix powder, for instance. Boss Fix powder, for example, is only effective for a boss inside the workplace, and will not affect the other employees. It is only effective against the boss who is cruel.

The bottom line is that nobody can be cursed without motive. The belief in this is founded upon the Bible especially Proverbs 26:2, that asserts that "an undeserved curse won't end."

The Book of Moses

An obscure influence on Hoodoo has to do with that of the "Sixth as well as the Seventh Book of Moses." This volume contains more than 100 articles which an Hoodoo adherent can apply to rituals of magic. Hex Signs that are listed in the book can be powerful symbolisms and talismans that can be used to shield one from strong curses. These can be sprayed on furniture, household items and other objects for protection of those who possess these items.

According to the legend that the story goes that it is believed that it was God who wrote the comprehensive guide to witchcraft to Moses on Mount Sinai, but it wasn't included in the Old Testament considering its power. The contents of the text reached the king Solomon and he took the advice to be one of the more influential and prominent people in the Christian religious system.

Stars and Their Spiritual Meanings

The celestial bodies are mysterious to this day even with all the information and technological advances we are equipped with. From the beginning of time, the nights have always provided a source of curiosity and fascination. It is easy to imagine the ways they enticed our forefathers, especially those African slaves chained and deprived from their freedom.

Not surprisingly, Hoodoo is a great source of influences from the stars as do many religions the mythological, and spiritual ones. It is all known under the term the science of astrology. The word "astrology" originates from the Greek terms "Astron," meaning "a star,"" as well as "logos," meaning "that is spoken of." This implies that the stars are actually containing God's words.

It's important to remember that astrology does not constitute a traditional Hoodoo method. The indications of the Zodiac and moon phases were frequently used in order to alter the duration of spells.

Zodiac Signs and How They Affect Intentions

Aries: The home of the self. New moons in Aries is about changing the ways of thinking and self.

Taurus is the house of wealth. It's the time to set goals for the wealth and money.

Gemini is the house of traveling. Gemini is a great sign to begin new adventures. Making your goals clear in this time will boost your chances of success.

Cancer is the home of families. Making plans in the event of a cancerous moon can help strengthen connections between families.

Leo is the house of romance. The lunar position in Leo is the ideal time to find the attention of a lover. This also boosts the likelihood of couples having the birth of a child.

Virgo is the House of Work. The intentions for career and work are well-suited during this time. Also, this is the ideal time to establish an exercise routine for example, an overhaul of your diet or fitness plan.

Libra House of connections. The fact that the new moon is located in the home of Libra signifies that it's time to strengthen the connections you have with your friends.

Scorpio is the house of mystery. If Moon is going to be in the astrological sign of Scorpio this is the ideal time for you to establish goals regarding the sharing of resources. It's a good time to resolve tax problems as well as the repayment of any debt.

Sagittarius The home of wisdom. A desire to expand your the horizon and exploring new areas are most beneficial. It's the ideal time to think about to go on a trip for the first time or enrolling in an online class on something you're unfamiliar with.

Capricorn is the house of the public. The most effective time to improve your image on the internet is during your moon aligns with the home of Capricorn. It could be a time to update your profile on the internet or updating your CV.

Aquarius is the home of friendship. It is the ideal time for setting goals to build on existing relationships or to meet new friends.

Pisces is the home of the dark. It is the ideal time to uncover your true self. Make a list of goals to make improvements and let go of others for a time.

Hoodoo oil plays a crucial part in the timings of the astrological calendar. Certain oils enhance the effect of moon's phases to the person taking the oil. Astral signs are also a crucial aspect of Hoodoo instructions. Hoodoo practitioners use stars as a guide. They represent the divine energy and followers direct their energies to specific stars based the goals they have set.

The Morning and Evening Stars

The Morning and Evening Stars refer to a unifying celestial body. There are two names for it due to the fact that it is visible at various dates, and some people were able to believe that the two were two different stars.

It is said that the Morning Star leads the sun to the dawn. It's a light source which carries wisdom and strength. As the sun goes down it is it is the Morning Star can be seen shining brightly alongside the sun and disappearing behind it at the sky.

It is believed that the star represents of Lucifer who's name translates to "bringer of the light."

Shooting Stars

Shooting stars are believed to be interpretable in different ways based on tradition of the. There are those who believe that they be a good luck charm, or an omen of good fortune. Many believe that it's the fate of a fallen angel. In Asian culture shooting stars can be interpreted as an indication of bad luck. The followers of Hoodoo determine the meaning based upon the culture they are part of.

Chapter 2: Hoodoo Ingredients And Materials

Hoodoo practices and spells contain dirt and dust. This is because they were easily accessible to those who first practiced Hoodoo. It is the Goofer dust, specifically is among the primary magic ingredients of Hoodoo.

Goofer Dust

Goofer is taken from the Bantu term 'kufua meaning "to be killed." The term is often utilized to hurt or kill the target. Goofer dust is made up primarily consisting of dirt from graveyards and dust but it can be made up of other elements based on the desired outcome. Two of the most common ingredients added to it are salt and snakeskin. They both provide a powerful method to inflict harm on the victim.

The dust can be spread across the victim's pillow or on the victim's route. The hex starts by creating sharp pains on the feet and legs of the victim. After that, the legs expand to the point that the patient can't move.

In time this practice changed to become a term called "goofering oneself," which is the way to cause harm by dispersing harmful elements throughout the area of victimization.

Graveyard Dirt

The Bokongo people from Central Africa were believed to initially used the graveyard soil to create spells. They believed that the dirt from graveyards held the spirit of deceased people. It is not possible to be simply taken it has to be purchased. The practitioner has to meet with the deceased and sign a written contract before. It is usually done by leaving gifts at the tomb of the deceased, in forms of items that the deceased enjoyed for example, alcohol, food or other objects.

Graveyard dirt does not have the same force. Graveyard dirt from infants and young children are considered to be particularly powerful in bringing luck and healing. In addition, dirt gathered from over the heart is frequently employed to create love spells.

Plants and Herbs

Herbs and plants are a key component of Hoodoo. Below is a listing of a few of the most popular ones employed in Hoodoo magic.

The Rose of Jericho

Sometimes referred to as the resurrection or false plant The Rose of Jericho originated from Mexico. It's brown, and extremely hard when it is dry. When it's immersed into the water, it spreads and turns vibrant. It becomes a holy plant that has flawless balance. The name of the plant indicates, it's utilized to cast spells in revitalizing a romantic relationship or to create a brand fresh one.

Horsetail

The horsetail plant is a lush and green one which is usually found in damp conditions. It is renowned for its healing and magical characteristics. If it is harvested correctly the herb can be used as an antifungal. If harvested in the incorrect time the product could be poisonous.

Basil

Basil is utilized in Hoodoo to bring good luck. It is a potent spell that attracts the love of your life or to bring about prosperity. It is also used to deflect negative vibes and bad spirits.

John the Conqueror

John the Conqueror is the name of a root med which has power that is traced through the ages of African American folklore. It is only necessary to be a part of it to enjoy the powers linked to luck and love. If you wear it in your hair, or the locks of someone that you like this person is likely to display admiration and interest for yourself as well.

Palo Santo

Palo Santo is regarded by the people of Hoodoo as being one among the most revered and potent plant species on earth. It's located throughout South America and is used by Shamans as well as healers. It is sometimes made into herbal teas that cleanse your body and strengthening immunity.

Cinnamon

Cinnamon is easily available and is a frequent component of a Hoodoo toolkit. It's a popular ingredient for sexually arousal as well as when used when sexually engaged, is believed to improve the sexual experience. In addition, cinnamon is believed to be a way to increase wealth and abundance.

Plants for Attracting Wealth

A lot of Hoodoo activities are based on the lure of cash. This is why a lot of the plants utilized in Hoodoo are the ones with the ability to attract money.

The Money Plant

Sometimes referred to as golden pothos this plant can be positioned in sharp angles inside the home to turn it into a space that is a place of achievement.

The Mother-in-Law Plant

The plant is often referred to by the name of snake plants. It's a plant that is healthy which is the natural cleansers as well as moisture.

Crassula

Crassula has succulent leaves. They can be employed in Hoodoo to provide a wealth of money to your home. It is recommended to place the plant in the southeast corner of the house for it to work.

Jasmine

The plant's aroma is utilized for attracting money and good fortune. The plant is also utilized to attract women.

Bamboo

Since the beginning of time Bamboo has been believed to be the source of good fortune and good health, specifically in Asian culture. Hoodoo believes in this belief and utilizes bamboo in the same way for this reason. Lucky bamboo, especially is utilized to bless the house.

Bayberry

The shrub grows in the parts of the eastern region of United States. If dried and blended the leaves can be utilized to bring prosperity and love.

Chamomile

Chamomile is known to treat and calm effects. Hoodoo's followers have used this daisy-like plant to boost prosperity and influence.

Sage

Sage is known to be powerful herb that purifies and reenergizes. In Hoodoo it is utilized not just for its curative properties however, it is also used for the ability it has to bring luck and romance.

Hoodoo Tools

Hoodoo devices are primarily an instrument to control the inner power of the individual. They do not have any magical power by themselves, and will not work without the intention of the individual who is using these tools. Certain users will only require minimum requirements, whereas others are looking for the most effective tools that are available. It all depends on the user's purpose.

Amulets and Charms

These devices produce energies as well as vibrations to both the receiver and the user. Though they appear as ordinary tools, they can be enchanting when used with the appropriate hands. It's essential that users keep candles in their holders also, as they play an crucial roles in some rituals.

The most powerful amulets are ones made by the individual who created them. They are made up of personal items including nails or hair clips which provide an extra boost of power.

Coyote Claws

Coyotes are a species that is known for their sly tactics. In spite of the stigma associated with this wild dog, it is thought to be in the best interests of mankind at its core. Coyotes are able to travel in the darkness and locate solutions in remote locations. The claws of coyotes are usually used by those who wish to be able to hide when travelling.

Porcupine needles

Porcupine needles are a great option to use in conjunction with dolls, rootswork and even candles. They are a great way to protect yourself and are usually placed near items that must be protected.

Incense

Incense is burned by practitioners when they perform rituals or spells. This can improve the enjoyment. Clay bowls are typically employed for burning incense, using charcoal self-igniting as a fuel source.

Incense Blends and Their Uses:

African Juju uses juju to draw arousing desire and love into a romance

Seven African Powers - an orisha essence that is used to get power from seven saints from Africa.

Banishing is a method of removing unwanted people from the life of a person.

Incense burns to bring harmony and peace within the house.

Chuparosa is also known as incense of the hummingbird, it is utilized to draw someone closer

Does not contain Hanna An incense that is utilized to boost Hoodoo tools.

Obeah This incense is smuggled to help people who are sorcerers or rootworkers to connect with spirits.

Jinx killer an incense blend which is smuggled to provide the protection against evil spirits and curses.

Dragon's blood, believed to be made up of real blood from dragons The resin is used to create power in rituals.

There are several companies that create and mixing incense like the ones listed above. They blend the formulas on demand.

Creating Your Formula

The creation of your own formulation can be necessary in order to develop strong rootswork. It is possible to mix herbs with other ingredients in order to create this. There are also powders and oils that are made to order.

Black Arts Oil

A powerful Hoodoo mixes, Black Arts Oil is employed to slay those who caused damage to yourself or those who you care about. The oil is made through the use of substances that are harmful, like snakeskin, red pepper as well as sulfur. They is then mixed with the herbal extracts of your preference.

Boss Fix Oil

Boss Fix Oil is a blend of ingredients that is designed to help people get who are in charge in the right position. The oil is usually placed on specific objects so that when the boss comes in contact with the object, they feel the pain or discomfort. This mixture could comprise high-john plants as well as licorice and plants, which is ideal for bosses who are abrasive to their employees.

Poppets

The traditional poppet dolls are made out of cloth or wax and are believed to represent spirits that are associated with the person who owns them. Many believe that poppets are akin to the voodoo dolls. But poppets aren't designed to harm anyone. If you make a pet, the shade of the material is what determines the strength the creature will have. Below is a list of the powers and colors that symbolize the power they represent:

Banishing Banishing Black fabric decorated with flames or swords.

Healing - Blue or white with a star or cloud decoration.

Innovation - Orange or yellow fabrics featuring sun or fire symbolism.

Hearts and Love - Rich red or pink fabric featuring bows, hearts, and hearts

Security - Red or white fabric decorated with shield or key embellishments.

Wealth Wealth Gold or silver fabrics that has green trims.

Various Hoodoo Tools

Lodestones

They are natural magnetized stones that are used to attract positive effects. They help to bring in lovers and money, and also to influence spells of other users.

Lucky Blue Balls

Sometimes referred to anil, these small balls composed of copper sulfate can be used to bring luck. They're dissolved in water to provide the cleansing effect.

Pyrite

Sometimes referred to as fool's gold and pyrite, it is a glistening substance that is commonly used to bring cash and bring success to its user.

Coins

Certain kinds of coins are employed to make use of certain types of coins in Hoodoo and most serve to bring luck to sufferers. These coins are not monetary and are usually sold at traditional stores.

Chapter 3: Hoodoo Spiritual Cleansing

The Hoodoo toolkit is the main component of the actual Hoodoo work. Therefore, the tools should be maintained physically and thoroughly. In addition, the person who is practicing is required to be clean spiritually throughout the day. The components used to cleanse are different based upon the process and needs of the individual practitioner, but there are common components to be used.

The importance of spiritual cleansing comes from many reasons. First, it lets the practitioner work in their highest capacity. Also, it eliminates any negative energy that could be attached to the practitioner or the surrounding environment.

Things To Include in a Cleansing Kit

Candles

Brick Dust

Salt

Chicken wings or Turkey wings

Chicken foot

Graveyard Dirt

Crystals

Holy Water

Essential oils

Alcohol Rub

Natural bath salts

Herbs such as rosemary, sage and palo santo sweetgrass, palo santo

Personal Cleansing

It is essential to cleanse your body, especially when you're feeling stressed or sick. There are likely to be instances where you'll feel like you're losing your energy or you may notice that there is a blockage in your energy. It is the ideal time to conduct a purification of your soul and body in order to restore your energy and levels of energy.

The act of performing this ritual during specific times of the day can increase the effectiveness of your ritual. It will increase the efficacy of the ritual. Ritual baths are particularly efficient for cleansing the aura to allow you to feel your strength for hours following.

If you'd like to be rid of rid of negativity take a bath using natural bath salts and essential oils, two cups of water that is blessed along with a few of your preferred herbs. Put two white candles on the edge of the bath and let them burn. Incorporate all the ingredients into the bath, to create a lively environment. Intake the bath once it has been filled.

Then, grab a small container and sprinkle the water on your head 13 times. Recite the prayer of cleansing. The most popular prayer is Psalm 37. You may also create an individual prayer. Only wash downwards so that the negative energy is sucked in the bath water.

After you've felt cleansed and refreshed, take a bath and let your hair air dry. Take care not to wash towels. Bring a tub full of bath water and bring it to a intersection. Then, throw the water by putting it on your back and walk home with no recollection.

Quick-Fix Methods

You have other options you could try, if you are unable to take a bath in order to clean your skin because of time limitations.

The Chicken Foot Lightly rubbing yourself by using your chicken's foot can aid in the removal of negative energy out of your. Much like a chicken can clean up the mess and get on with your day.

Brushing: If you need to do a more intense cleaning, you can make use of a chicken or turkey wings instead. Pick up the turkey wing, and use it to brush the head's top all the way to your feet. This can be a way of getting rid of any problem.

Rubdown - This involves making use of alcohol as the base. The mixture is infused by adding oils and herbs prior to rubbing it onto yourself. Make it more enjoyable by doing the ceremony in a sacred space and with chants and prayers.

Candle - You could use an unlit candle to eliminate an unlucky condition. Cleanse yourself using the candle downward movements while praying an affirmation.

Smoke - Making use of smoke for cleansing can be described as smudging. This can be done using dried herbal teas, essential oils or incense. You can cover yourself in white fabric starting from your neck and then burn whatever that you like. The smoke will be circulated around you, then remove the cover to allow it to spread throughout the space.

Sprinkler Heads - A sprinkler could also be utilized to purify. It is filled with holy or holy water, mixed with essential oils and salt. Make sure to saturate your shoulders and head as you recite your favourite. Do not forget to dust your feet.

Cleansing and Blessing the Home

Floor washes made from the same items that are that are used for personal cleaning could be utilized for the cleaning of the home as well as other locations. The washing guidelines apply to all of them, including ensure that the water is directed down to draw all negative energy to the ground and eliminate negative luck. Smudging, prayers, as well as candles are a great option for deeper cleansing.

Practitioners typically use essential ingredients to boost the effectiveness of blessing and cleansing.

Earth

The most basic form in Earth is dirt that comes from the earth. If you're not keen to utilize actual dirt alternative options are available to employ in place.

Redbrick dust - This type of Earth is thought to work and is commonly sprinkled around such as windows, doors as well as entrances and thresholds. It is the most potent form that's typically found in holy constructions and ancient houses.

For creating mental barriers that are incomparable create unbroken lines along your success's horizons. Do this on the time of the full moon to get a more effective result. Make sure you clean the dust each month.

Salt It's a very common element due to its availability. It's also simple to get rid of. Sea salt has a particular effectiveness and is frequently used in fighting bad dreams and nightmares. In order to get rid of sleep problems, you can sprinkle areas around your bed with regular salt or sea salt. The placement of a large container full of salt by the doorway can also protect your residence from the negative energy.

Black Salt - This salt is made up of regular salt and sea salt. It also has charcoal as well as iron filling. It is used to deal especially strong negative energies.

Air

Air is a component which is naturally used during house purifications and blessings. You can use it with candles or incense while the windows and doors are open to allow negative energy go.

Fire

Black and white candles can be utilized to boost the power of cleansing your house. The strength of these candles is enhanced by mixing the essential oils for example, Sandalwood as well as Myrrh.

Water

The deep cleansing of homes is made up of the element. This element can cleanse the body of ailment. Nowadays, it is possible to acquire healthy water by purchasing these items at stores selling Hoodoo products.

It is also possible to improve the quality of your own water by this method:

Step 1: Take just enough seawater to be used to cleanse yourself. Make sure you give a token of appreciation to those spirits who reside within the water body from the place you took the water.

2. Gather rainwater. The ideal rainwater is that collected by a storm

Step 3: Let the water that you've collected over night in the light of the moon. Mix rainwater and seawater inside a glass container. Set the container outside on a table so that it receives the greatest amount of moonlight. It should be charged with prayer and prayers before letting it go. the container overnight.

Step 4. Add salt to the water. The holy salt is a good choice. The water is stirred by turning it clockwise as you add the salt, and pray.

Cleansing Spells to Eliminate Toxicity

The environment that we live in is filled with negative energy. That's the reason it's so important to cleanse certain areas of negative energy and anger. These spells have been designed specifically for focusing on the intention and not an overall cleansing ritual.

Moonlight Spell

To perform this ritual for this spell, you'll need the white candle, incense and some soothing music.

For the first time cleanse yourself in the evening after the full moon. Dress in a white robe following drying yourself with air.

Find a calm spot outdoors or near the window so that it is possible to see directly the moon.

Relax with some soothing music and then light the incense.

Contact your spiritual guide and ask them to safeguard your spirit's vitality and provide your body with healing power.

Let the energy flow as it moves through you through the soles of your feet all the way to the top of your head.

In this time start to forgive yourself for the mistakes you have made and begin feeling that the burdens of life to take over yourself.

Then, you should thank the universe for the good fortune it has provided you. You can also acknowledge your angels or spirits for the assistance they have provided.

Spell for the Soul

If you are feeling that your spirit is weighed down and burdened, get back in control by the use of this magic spell. It includes a white candle holy salt, dried sage blessed water and an herb bowl to burn.

Pick a date with a dim moon for this magick. First, light the candle and ask the spirit to help bless your ceremony. Your hand should be swept through the flame and then recite "I make use of the fire to dispel negativity within and I request that they be replaced by positive goals."

Then, rub the holy salt in your palms. Recite "Through this component, I surrender any negative element in my personal life."

Following that, ignite the sage you have dried up in the bowl. Breathe into the smoke. Repeat, "With the element of air, I purify my spirit and purge any thoughts that disturb me."

Immerse your hands in the water, and repeat, "I use water to remove toxins from my body and to bring positive and clear goals to my heart."

The ritual is complete. Get rid of the various ingredients that you have used by mixing the salt and incense. Then, dissolve them in water and then scatter it over an intersection or place it beneath the tree.

Chapter 4: Hoodoo Mojo Bag

Utilizing a bag for mojo is among the most effective methods to enhance your magical practices, and also make these bags personally chargeable. Mojo bags can also be referred to as conjuring bags, toby or condition bags. They also include gris-gris. There's no limit to the number of mojo bags you'd prefer to possess. They can be customized to meet your requirements and tastes.

The Mojo bags function as batteries which keep your power fully charged. So, you should take them along with you everywhere. Bags for commercial use are readily accessible, however a hand-crafted bag is a great way to improve your connection to the magical sources.

The colour plays a significant factor when selecting a material to fill the mojo bags. Some fabrics, such as satin or deep velvets are popular alternatives, and for others there is muslin, cotton or even muslin.

Silver-This color is associated in conjunction with the moon. It is associated with the goddess of yin, who encourages peace and calm.

Gold - Gold is aligned with the sun to bring wealth and prosperity. The god yang can be connected to gold. It is an energetic and powerful type of energy.

Red The color red Red has a connection to Mars and symbolizes the power of passion and courage. The more intense the color of red it is, the more powerful your mojo.

Violet The color Violet symbolizes healing. Also, it aids in spiritual connections. By using these colors, your instruments are able to work when making divine connections or a connection to the realm of spirit.

Orange is associated with Mercury and symbolizes the success. It supplies all the elements in the bag, bringing energy and velocity.

Blue Blue Blue is closely associated with Jupiter. Choose this color for your purse if you wish to increase the wisdom of your magic.

Yellow - Yellow is controlled by the sun. It represents happiness and creativity. It can bring a sense of attraction to your spells.

Green The color of green Green is associated in conjunction with Venus and ensures that your bag is infused with prosperity and wealth.

Rose Pink - The color of friendship and love. rose pink can be employed to improve creative and romantic talents.

Grey Gray Tools contained in a gray mojo bag can be used to create illusions. They are useful when applied to secret actions and spells that require invisible.

White Color - White is a symbol of divination and spirituality. Bags that are white helps you connect to spiritual beings. This bag will also to improve your mental health.

Black is a powerful color. Black increases the effectiveness of casting spells to banish. Associated with Saturn Black, it can bring discipline for the person who is practicing.

How to Make Your Mojo Bag

1. Measure the fabric, then cut it in order to create a rectangle three times wider than the length. If, for instance, you're looking to create a 12 inch long rectangle you can make it 4 inches broad.

Step 2. Fold the cloth into two pieces so it is that one side faces the outside, while the smooth side is faces inside. Set the edges and ends following and trim any excess.

Step 3. Sew along to the sides. Leave the remaining two inches unfinished to make the pocket. The top of the pocket will be the pocket, therefore keep it unsown.

Step 4. The bag should be turned inside-out and make sure it is facing outwards. The smooth surface of the bag is looking outwards. Unfold the fabric into a flap both sides of the bag.

Step 5: With the scissors you have Make four tiny cuts along the fold you've just created.

Step 6. Thread a tiny ribbon or string of color through the slits. Make sure that it's long enough to wrap around the body of the bag, leaving extra length for tie-tying.

Step 7. Charge your bag by putting crystals, stones, herb along with other items so that it can serve its purpose. to serve.

Step 8: Tie the strings of your bag tightly to keep your things safe and safe. In this time it is your turn decide which items you're keeping inside your mojo bag. It will be based upon the goal you're aiming for. In general, bags for mojos contain different objects because odd numbers are thought of as to be active and dynamic. In addition, the total number of items in the bag should not be more than 13 as this will cause the bag to be less efficient.

Fill your bag up with relevant things. It is possible to place gemstones, herbs, or amulets as well as personal belongings that signify your intention.

Utilize obsidian arrowheads, the lodestone and basil as well as a shield amulet to guard yourself.

Pack your bags with three leaves of clover, lucky coins the rabbit's foot as well as dry John the Conqueror for luck.

To achieve wealth and prosperity Keep a lodestone in a container with John the Conqueror root, the tumbled tiger-eye crystals and a selenite twig.

To draw attention to your partner, you can place in your bag rosehips and magnetic sand containing hearts of rose quartz and dried petals, and an article of paper with an expression of love.

Then, put the dried root along with an alligator claw, Agate crystal, as well as magnetized salt in your bag to aid in the purpose of lifting or crossing a cross.

Once you've sorted everything you require within bags, final step is to blessing the bag. Make sure to blow through the opening of your bag and praying to God: "With my breath, I pray for you just like the Lord breathed into all living things and breathed life into everyone." Pull the cord close to lock the bag in place and the contents. Make sure your bag is sprayed with fixes dots or sprays of magical oil. Put a dots at each corner and another on the middle.

Grab your bag, and then make a prayer "I pray for you and I give your goals (state the purpose you have set for yourself) as well as I secure you to me and provide you with the strength to succeed."

After that, you have to make your point clear by using the magic candle. Make a note of your goal on a candle that you can attach it using nine pins. Make sure you insert the pin that is the final one through the wick before you light the candle and then stating the intention to repeat the intention.

You can give your mojo bag the name you want and turn it into the physical embodiment of your spiritual friend. Hoodoo devotees don't see their bags as mere physical instruments that are not alive. The bag that you use to carry your mojo is part of you. Naming it will allow you to identify a persona and energy to it.

How Long Does a Mojo Bag Retain Its Power?

Mojo bags last for a minimum of a year. If you want to keep your bag functioning make sure you secure it in a way that only you as the owner is able to see the contents. If anyone else is able to see or gets into your bag it could cause it to become useless.

If you've got any hard-to-clean items that are kept in your bag ensure that you take off and scrub every once in awhile. Things that are soft like flowers or herbs need to be cleaned whenever needed.

Chapter 5: Conjure Work

Conjure is a blend of different cultures. Hoodoo's conjure art incorporates African traditions, as well as the Protestant base Germanic, East European cultural influences, as well as the traditional folklore about herbs of Native Americans.

It's crucial to recognize the fact that conjure magic is the spiritual practice built on the established folk magic of Hoodoo. There are two kinds of work that conjure that are based on learning and wisdom. The first is founded on the traditional methods that are passed through generations from one generation to one generation to. A more formal form of stream includes studying different forms of intellectual magic.

Traditionally, conjure physicians learned about themselves by studying of magic from books that contained spiritual and magical knowledge drawn from various civilizations. The texts were published from grimoires, as well as other books that contained old-fashioned spells.

Conjuring is a process that involves roots and candles and the blending of natural elements to create salves, oils as well as powders.

The Right Time to Perform Conjuring

The best time to use your conjuring skills is at any time you're required to. There isn't any set rules on the best time to utilize the technique. They can be used at whenever and at any time you want to do so, in line with your wishes and desires. It is important to recognize, however, that the influence of the moon can greatly enhance the quality of the quality of work you do.

The Full Moon

Full moons are viewed as a time of prosperity and development. When it starts to fade and shrink, it becomes smaller before fading away into darkness. If you have a particular subject or object that you would like to eliminate then you should use a particular ritual to eliminate that person out of your life.

First thing to complete is writing down the name of the person or object on a clean piece of paper. Take a chunk of lemon and cut the lemon into a small hole. Place the lemon on the newspaper and then cover it with a small piece from red pepper.

Make the hole with a black thread. Pray to the god of your choice or saint for the ability to liberate yourself from the person prior to the full moon.

Repetition your prayer over the next 15 days, and look for clues. Hoodoo will provide signals to assist you in reaching the goal you set for yourself. It's just a matter of being aware and follow the direction it shows you.

Charging Your Lucky Talisman

Hoodoo does not normally rely on moonlight to increase the strength of ingredients utilized in spells, rituals, and rituals. The ingredients themselves are strong enough, and need only to be replenished by using salt. The moon's role is just increase the power of the mojo bag and other luck charms. Charge these charms during the night of the new moon is an individual event and not intended to be shared with anyone else.

Moonlight is the ideal time to perform rituals. We humans can be affected by the power of moonlight. But, when we invoke the powers of the moon, it is the person who is conjuring, not from the moon.

The Powder of Powders

The most powerful powders are the essential ones which every magician has in their arsenal. The powders are used to create various types of magic. It is possible to use them for powering mojo bags and dress wallets. They can also be used as magic love potions that can attract lovers, as well as repel others away from your daily living. These potions can also be utilized to get rid of jinxes, and also bring prosperity and wealth.

Aphrodite Powder

The ideal time to create this powder is at New Moon.

To make this powder you'll require:

Pomegranate seeds

Organic cocoa powder

Dried mango skins

Dried apple skins

Tea leaves of Hibiscus

Hibiscus petals

Rose petals

Tea leaves of Chamomile

Passionflower essential oil

Utilize a mortar and pestle to crush all of these ingredients into the form of a small powder. Add a couple of drops of essential oils from passionflower and then store the finished substance in glass bottles.

The Wild West Powder for Crossing or Banishing

The ideal time to create this substance is during waxing moon.

To make this powder you'll require:

3 cloves of black

Powdered onion

Red cayenne powder

Cumin seeds

Fresh Paparika

Ground black pepper

Oil from Red Hot Chili

Mix the ingredients using an ordinary blender. It is also possible to crush the ingredients with your fingers. The final product can be stored in a container that is sealed, ensure that you wash your hands before you handle the product.

Hard Cash Powder

The most effective time to apply this powder is if the full moon is on a Thursday, and the day has either an 8 or 7 in the date. It can be utilized to draw wealth and money or to improve your odds of winning when you gamble.

To make this powder you'll require:

Cloves

Tea leaves of Chamomile

Fresh ginger

Dry leaves of a potentilla flower

Dried nutmeg

Fresh mint

A four-leaf clover

Lavender essential oil.

Mix all the ingredients and then add a few drops of essential oils before placing in the glass bottle.

Algiers Powder

The powder can be employed to make a dusting of the body to attract love. The best time to use it is when the moon is full.

For making this powder you'll need:

Dried rose petals

Deadnettle leaves

Orris roots

Vanilla essential oil

Blend all ingredients, then incorporate into base flour.

Dream Powder

Make use of it if you're looking to dream of prophetic visions and create a connection with spirits while you sleep. This can be used best when the moon is in a waxing phase.

For making this powder you'll need:

Cinnamon powder

Cardamom seeds

Coriander seeds

Tea leaves of Licorice

Ginger

Blend all ingredients, then make a base flour. Dust the powder on the sheets and pillowcases before you go to sleep.

Jinx Removal Powder

The most effective time to create this substance is during a dim moon.

For the production of this powder you'll need:

Dry wintergreen leaves

Tea leaves of Chamomile

Fresh mint leaves

Essential oil Citric

Mix the ingredients into an emulsion and then add it either to a rice-flour or the base of cornstarch.

Controlling Powder

Make use of this when you need to control other people.

To make this powder you'll need:

Epsom salts

Magnetic Sand

Saltpeter that has been dried

Myrrh

Combine all the ingredients and then incorporate into a base of flour.

Cascarilla Powder

The powder can be used to make the appearance of a protective circle. It is a great way to cleanse and secure your house when it is added to an aeration wash for floors. It is only necessary to have eggshells for this process. Cleanse the eggshells, and dry them completely before pulverizing them to create an extremely small powder.

Oils

Conjure Oil

It's an all-purpose oil, which is utilized to boost the power of your work with conjuring. Use it to increase your ability and bring your dreams into reality.

In order to make this oil it is necessary to:

Equal parts lotus-scented oil

Equal parts of Frankincense

Equal portions Sandalwood

Combine all three ingredients, and then store it in an glass bottle.

Good Luck Oil

There is a need for an oil base from Jojoba oil to create a an oil of good luck. After you've got an oil base it is possible to add it:

Three drops oil from cinnamon

15 drops essential lavender oil

20 drops Gaultheria Oil

For making the oil more financially-focused You can mix in ginger and vetiver oil.

Confusion Oil

This oil is utilized for helping your adversaries fight one with each.

In order to make this oil you'll need:

1 equal amount patchouli oil as well as 1 equal portion chili pepper oil

Include the following ingredients in the oil mix:

*Blackened chili peppers (bell green, red, chili)

Grains of heaven

Poppy seeds

Mustard seeds

Additionally, you can mix in dried vitamin E for a stronger oil.

Van Van Oil

This is one of the most well-known recipes ingredient, and has been passed down through generations. Certain ingredients could be a challenge to locate however, their absence will not alter the quality of the oil in any way.

For the production of this oil it is necessary to:

2 drops of palmarosa oils

16. Drops of oil from lemongrass

32 drops citronella oil in the form of drops

This is your oil of base and you may mix in various other ingredients. You can, for instance, use essential oils as well as dried herbs. Be sure to dilute the solution with the cleanest carrier oil before making use of it.

Other Types of Conjuring

Hoodoo professionals don't claim to know better than doctors who are professional. However, at the similar time they are aware the fact that certain natural ingredients serve as treatment for specific conditions.

Headache Salve

In order to make this salve you'll need:

1 cup light organic oil (sesame oil or sunflower oil)

1/2 oz pure beeswax

White Sage

Lavender

Eucalyptus

Vitamin E (liquid)

Strainer

These ingredients may be fresh or dried the choice is your choice what proportions of each you'd like to incorporate. Start with one ounce at a time and then make changes along the method.

Put all the herbs in an oven-proof dish. Cover them with oil. The mixture is baked at 180°C for 3 hours, then allow it to cool for about 30 minutes afterward. Then, remove the herbs and strain out any excess liquid by using an edging cloth.

Pour the infused herbal oil into a stainless steel pot, and let it simmer at a low temperature for around 10 minutes before including vitamin E.

Include beeswax in the mixture and heat it until the liquid is completely melted.

The pot should be removed and allowed to allow the mixture to sit for five minutes. Just before the mixture is set and is ready to be decanted into different bottles and allow it to cool. When the salve is cool and has thickened, seal the containers of bottles. Apply the salve to ease headaches. Spread a thin layer over your forehead or temples.

Wasps Nest Conjuring

The remains of a dead wasp's nest could be used to conjure. If you find one, don't toss the nest away. To create a nest of wasps conjuring, you need to grind the nest, then incorporate it into the hex or banishing powders.

Hoodoo experts believe that nests of wasps have potent protection abilities, and the sacred teachings of Treemonisha which is also known as the dirt dauber's nest.

Mix a portion of the nest with warm water as well as goofer dust to make an encapsulating mixture. If you're looking to build a mix that permits you to penetrate the lives of another, a the wasp nest is a crucial component.

Enhancing Your Conjure Work

Spiritual healers understand and acknowledge how powerful words as well as speech. They are aware of how words be a powerful tool to increase the effectiveness of intentions. In particular, the Holy Scriptures, in particular as well as prayers is believed to be the strongest kind of incantation which can provide strength to the spirits.

Hoodoo attaches importance on the Bible because it is stuffed with information useful to the reader and is in line with the principles of Hoodoo rituals.

Important Psalms Use for Strengthening Conjure Work

Psalm 51. This Psalm can be used to cleanse and often paired as a part of healing baths. This is a powerful text that contains prayerful incantations for the removal of all iniquities and sinning. Utilize this Psalm in case you feel you need to re-establish your faith in God or find salvation.

Psalm 64 The Psalm is mostly used to provide security. The Psalm calls on God to guard against individuals with evil motives. You can recite it anytime you feel you're under threat or are ready to speak up against people who oppress you.

Chapter 6: The Use Of Candle Magic

Candles are used for a long time to aid in spiritual and religious practices. Egyptians use candles for millennia. The Romans have also utilized them during their celebrations. Buddhists as well, made use of candles to make candles using animal fat.

The early Hoodoo members are often described as using candles to perform their duties However, in actual fact those who took part in Hoodoo did not have access to candles. First, they were priced too high and could only be seen at the homes of the wealthy.

After their liberation Former slaves traveled around and formed groups. They also promoted candles as the primary element of Hoodoo rituals. In the late 1940s, several booklets were released that encouraged the use of different kinds of candles in Hoodoo practice. Nowadays, candles are well-known among novices.

The Meaning of Candle Colors

The early Hoodoo people didn't understand their significance in the diverse colours the candles symbolized. The primary colors they were working with were white and black, both representing good and evil and evil, respectively. In the modern age, as Hoodoo changed and evolve, so did the ideas and rituals.

Some cultures believe that the colour of a candle can create psychic connections and resonates however that's not necessarily the case for Hoodoo. Magic and strength come not in the actual candle however, but the intentions. However, there were instances when Hoodoo users utilized colored candles mostly to keep their minds on track of what they were doing in order not to get distracted.

White Candles They are utilized for blessings and healing. White candles are the first candles that were used in the traditional Hoodoo.

Black Candles These are used to place hexes on or around people.

Red Candles They represent blood. Blood is the life-force that is present in all living creatures and red candles are strong as well. They represent the desires concerning love and romance. They can also symbolize boldness and audacity.

Pink Candles These candles use pink to bring focus on family issues. It symbolizes friendship and respect among families. The color is also utilized for treating wounds that have been caused by the spirit and to bring back positive energies within the spirit.

Blue Candles The candles that are burnt to create joy. Blue is a color that symbolizes peace and harmony, and it can bring harmony for families.

Gold Candles Gold candles are utilized to bring fortune as well as wealth.

Orange Candles They are used to create doorways, and eliminate obstacles. They can be used to make pathways to success as well as improving concentration.

Yellow Candles The candles symbolize the changing of fortune and change. They help make situations which can change the lives of those affected.

Green Candles Green means material gain. Green candles help with magic which can be directed towards business issues as well as help boost financial position.

The Gray and Silver Candles Both of them are beneficial in casting spells to provide security. They can be burned to ease grief and pain caused by loss or grieving.

Purple Candles symbolize mastery. This candle is ideal if you wish to increase your power by casting an intention for controlling others.

Brown Candles Burned for the purpose of ensuring the success of legal proceedings.

Hoodoo Candle Terminology

Here's a listing of candles and terms that are used to describe the art of Hoodoo:

Costumed Candles: When making candles dressed, people use substances to guide spirits towards their goals. Ideally, you should choose candles that signalize your intent, after that, apply oils and roots to enhance the magic. If you want to draw security, as an example it is best to use an uncolored candle, and then protect it by covering it with oil. Additionally, you can mix several kinds of oils to improve the appearance of your candle.

Do not over-load the candle with oil because it could ignite it. Decorate your candle with 4 to 5 drops of oils.

Fixed Candles Fixed are comparable to candles that are dressed, except that they're made by others. They are filled with oils and herbs after a prayerful process. The candles are also packed with dedication.

A Loaded Candles They are candles which have been cut into the shape of a cylinder and then filled with herbs oil, roots and other substances. It is possible to make your own candle loaded with ingredients according to your preferences or purchase one that's already been made.

Carved Candles Carving candles is employed to channel magic towards an individual or object. Carve the name of someone and use your magic to target the person. These symbols are representative of the way you would like your magic to work. Eye symbols can, for example, mean security.

The Rolled Candles are candles that have been rolled with herbs and oil. They appear impressive, but they can cause harm as the herb may influence how the candles burn. A few elements could be blown off, causing fire.

Be aware that all kinds of candles employed in Hoodoo can be risk to ignite and should be handled with caution. Make sure to use candles that are encased whenever you can as they are more secure and more likely to not be caught on fire.

Figure Candles

Form candles, also known as effigy candles aren't part of the traditional Hoodoo as are colored candles. They're a brand new idea and do not intend to portray spirits or other people, however they can be used to remind the person of their purpose.

Many people believe that the novelty candles are only bringing Hoodoo to the forefront of the spotlight. Some believe that they improve rituals. The most effective way to allow the Hoodoo participant to make a decision is to study the candle, and then decide by themselves what the meaning of the candle is.

Skull Candles The candles symbolize the mind. They can be employed to influence thoughts and influence the way you would like another to act. The shade of the candle dependent on the intent of the person who is using it. White skulls work best for alleviating grief for people grieving.

Satanic Candles Also called Satan candles These candles are positioned inside windows and doors to eliminate bad spirits from your home.

Seven Knob Candles can be powerful candles featuring seven indentations. They're designed to last seven days. You could make use of them to ask for a specific thing for the duration of seven days or you can wish to have seven different things happen in one go.

Baphomet Sabbatical Goat Goat is a symbol of authority and power The candle used to force persons in non-sexual issues. Use these candles anytime you'd like to influence others' thoughts.

Cat-Shaped Candles Cats are believed to bring luck and prosperity. Use these candles to draw luck.

Money Pyramid Candles They symbolize money and power, and are typically decorated with the eye of all-seeing. They protect your possessions as well as the house from harm as well as theft.

Wedding Pyramid Candle an image-based candle that depicts the picture of a couple who are in love. The candle is designed to increase the romance and love.

How to Read Candle Burning

The meaning of a flamed candle is a matter of interpretation. It could mean a variety of things according to the materials that is used to make the candle as well as its wick. If you want to master the art candle reading, it is important make sure that you buy the candle from the same source each time in order to ensure the flame stays steady.

Candles should be made by yourself at least to be sure of the quality you're receiving.

Hoodoo is your aid to achieving the results it thinks you should get. If you burn a poor constructed candle and receive an omen that leads your on a new path take a moment to accept what you were expecting to be. When you get better at your craft the interpretation of messages are going to become a second-nature thing for you.

The Meaning Behind Candle Flames

There are many ways that a candle burns with their own significance. If you are burning your magical candles make sure that the flame is burning in a consistent manner and doesn't get affected by the drafts.

An upwardly slanting flame indicates that things are good.

If a flame is bouncing, it indicates that somebody is trying to get in touch with you immediately. It's not necessarily a negative sign, and may mean that spirits are encouraging your efforts.

If the flame is dancing or flickers across the room with a steady rhythm this means your energy levels are exploding. The flame is signaling you to slow down and focus on getting free of any distracting thoughts.

A flame shrinking means you are lacking vitality. If this occurs, it signifies that you're getting slower to achieve your goals and desires.

An increased flame sends contradictory messages. This could indicate that the task will be finished much faster, however it may also mean that the outcomes of your work are not lasting long.

The blue flame usually signifies that you're on right path and you have a better probability of achieving.

Green flames indicate the wealth. It doesn't necessarily mean cash, but it does mean that everything you'd like to have will appear abundantly.

The presence of white smoke is an excellent sign that signifies that you are doing well with your job.

The black smoke indicates resistance. Somebody is trying to stop you which means you should stop the task and apply a road opening or blockage spell prior to resuming according to your present plan.

How to Read Candle Wax

Candle wax reading in Hoodoo is known as ceromancy. The practice involves interpreting the flow of wax through an unburned candle. If the candle has been encased correctly and placed on a level surface your interpretation and reading will be much more precise.

The candle's wax looks like tears of a human This could indicate tears are shed due to the work you've done. If the pattern stops prior to the candle has gone out this means that the pain is temporary.

Pinnacles When the candle's wax does not get to the bottom of the candle, or it breaks off, this means that someone who is involved in your spells may be seeking to hold onto the old past. The person could have issues to deal with, and that could affect your efforts.

Absence of wax dips signifies that you have succeeded. That means that the work you did was done perfectly and you'll succeed.

If the spread of wax appears uneven as a puddle, that's an indication that your desire was granted. But, it could also mean there are more paths which you'll have to follow and the work you've done isn't completed.

A slick of white wax on one side indicates that there is something different going on. This could make your spell unfinished, and could be a sign of unbalanced energy in your soul.

How to Read Wax Puddles

Candle wax must create a form that's obvious when you're doing specific rituals. For example, puddles with a heart shape symbolize romance. Other patterns can signify there's something wrong with the world.

Remains of claws that resemble remnants suggest they are a sign that someone has spread stories and gossip about your. It is recommended to repeat the work until you can see the wax glowing smoothly.

Puddles of wax that look like the genitalia can indicate troubled relationships or unfaithfulness.

The appearance of wax pillars that don't look natural or look like a representation of beasts indicate that the spell was not effective due to external disturbances. Make use of some powder oil to remove these harmful effects.

Puddles of wax that look like coffins indicate the hex or jinx spells you've used were successful and the threat against you was defeat.

Chapter 7: Rootwork

The slaves were deprived of their liberty and had next or no influence on their lives. But, even though masters of the slaves had physical body, they were not able to be a part of their souls. They remained in control of their spirits and utilized their imaginations to keep their hopes and energy high, particularly during toughest time.

The famous character High John developed a reputation in the time of slavery, inspiring slaves by telling stories about his exploits and the ways they were able to defeat his master. The name he is most well-known as High John the Conqueror, large man who utilized the art of trickery and skill to evade working.

There is a legend it is believed that High John was an African prince that was sold to slaves. Others say that he was the commoner. Whatever his background He was known for his capacity to stay out of the rigors of. He was an incredibly strong individual and luck was always at his side. He was renowned for his ability to beat the opposition even when the latter would be a fool.

The High John is linked to Ipomea Jalapa, which is the most potent root that is often found in the Hoodoo magician's bag. Many practitioners use High John Root to remove barriers and defeat their opponents. Incorporating it into the mojo bag in green increases the lucky factor. This will help bring money to the owner.

Popular Roots and Herbs in Hoodoo

Angelica Root Also called Archangel root. If you place dried Angelica roots on all four corners in your residence and it protects your property from harm. This root can be used to boost the purification process or the removing of Hexes. Additionally, this root can assist in the rekindling of lost love.

Bats Head Root Also referred to as Ling nut, horny Bulls head as well as Devil pod, the bats head root is a bit like the skull of a devil. You can use it at any time you'd like the desires of your heart to be fulfilled and eliminate any obstruction to your path.

Blood Rot Root The root may serve multiple functions. It is a great way to resolve marriage and family conflicts as well as improve sexual relations in the process at the time. time. By burning it at the time of a ceremony, you will stop someone else from acquiring your partner. Also, you can place it in the windows to draw potential lovers.

Calamus Root Burn this root in conjunction with other kinds of tasks to boost the power of the initial spell. It's a powerful root that can boost the effectiveness of your spell whatever the circumstance.

Devils Shoestring Root This root could be utilized to improve the odds of getting the perfect job. This root can also assist in your present job. Use it when looking for job or want to control sexuality of the other sexe.

Fennel Place this plant on your office or at home to keep away negative energy and bad spirits. This is especially beneficial for females and is able to attract riches and money for them.

Hazel It is used in the making of fertility amulets. Put some twigs in your windows to shield the lightning from striking.

Lavender is a herb that brings peace and a sense of sexual pleasure for couples that are having difficulties in the bedroom. Sometimes, it is utilized to protect against domestic abuse Rub it onto the victim and it acts as a shield.

Magnolia The blossoms of the Magnolia flower are used by men to attract women. The flower can also be utilized to attract fidelity and stop the partners from seeking another lover.

Nutmeg The Nutmeg is a lucky plant and a favourite among gamblers. The herb can draw luck and fortune as well as a sign of wealth.

Galangal Root, also called The Chewing John root It is an effective guarding root, which can be chewed during casting reverse Hex-type spells. It is then disposed of to remove hex magic out of your daily life. If you're in the midst of an upcoming court hearing, you should use Galangal root to burn at least two weeks prior to the day of trial to ensure success. Also, you can use this root to draw the wealth. Wrap money in it and it'll do the work.

Ginger Hoodoo considers ginger as one of the top and flexible rootstocks. Ginger is utilized to boost confidence, sexuality, and wealth. Ginger can increase the power of your roots and improve the outcome.

The Queen Elizabeth Root This is an powerful root that is employed to invoke sexual sex and love. It's also referred to as an orris plant, and is able to attract the opposite gender and boost the likelihood of lasting romance. The leaves are sprinkled onto the sheets prior to making love and utilized to improve marriages and boost fertility.

Hyssop It is a purifying herb which has been utilized for a considerable time. It's a potent herbal remedy for cleaning the home and eliminating Hexes.

Five Finger Grass is sometimes referred to as the cinquefoil. It can be used to attract wealth and achieving the success. By bathing in the water with five fingers of grass, you'll be capable of getting rid of some of curses.

Licorice Root Licorice can be utilized to influence the thoughts of someone else or change the way they think.

Mugwort Artemisia vulgaris, also known as mugwort, is a specific root that can be used to cleanse magical devices such as crystals and talismans. It can neutralize negativity and to restore the strength and power of the instruments.

Parsley In Hoodoo the use of parsley in Hoodoo is to help promote calm and peace within the household. Parsley can also be utilized to protect food from food borne illness. In addition, it can be employed to assist in healing after surgeries or illnesses.

The Pepper Tree Pepper tree is a potent herb that is used to protect. It also has properties for healing also, and could aid in recovering those who've undergone operations.

Thyme is a herb that assists in increasing psyche-boosting power as well as cleansing the rootwork. It helps you gain understanding and courage to keep going with your task.

Witch Hazel Bark A product used by Native Americans to Hoodoo, which is utilized for healing the oral and skin problems. In rootwork sessions the bark can help increase chastity and decrease emotions. It's good to have this bark in belongings when you're grieving may assist in decreasing the grief.

Creating Talismans and Amulets Using Herbs and Roots

The word "talisman" is a reference to the fact that Talisman or amulet is not exactly the same thing. It is an artificial item that has energy. It can be made from different materials, and are typically placed around the neck, or on fingers to form rings. Additionally, they can be embellished using natural materials including stones and crystals.

On contrary is a natural item that is able to be consecrated or blessed to conjure or perform magic. They can also be charged with intent, based on the needs of users require.

How to Create an Amulet

Amulets are usually made from sturdy materials like stones or gems. Hag stone is one the most commonly used elements to create amulets. The hag stone is a stone with holes that are created by water running through it.

The design of the stone you pick indicates what its power is. For example, a heart-shaped stone can be used for spells of love. In contrast stones that resemble daggers can be utilized to protect yourself. You can make your amulet more wearable with natural fibers and cords to put it on the neck or around your wrist.

Make use of sacred salt in water to purify and cleanse the amulet. It will eliminate any negativity or contaminants from your amulet. Dry it naturally, then go through the inhalation of the herbs you have chosen until you can feel the amulet is recharged.

The process of charging an amulet could include calling upon the gods you trust to protect your life and grant you power and love.

How to Create a Talisman

In order to create a talisman it is first necessary to select an object that is the focus. It can be a necklace or a ring you have. Keys, coins, and other similar metal items are a great way to make your Talisman.

After you've selected the object you want to use, consider what you intend to do with it. will be.

Will you make use of it to protect yourself? Are you planning to use it for attracting love? Select the most suitable time in the month to begin working on the talisman that will enhance its effectiveness. Look up the lunar calendar to determine which time is the most suitable time to get started on the design.

For a talisman that is practical, try using leather straps which allow the wearer to put the talisman on the waist or around your neck. Make use of herbs and roots to make an infusion enhance your talisman. Apply several drops each day and ensure that the item is kept in an safe location.

The talisman is charged with the energy of your body, allowing the force of your desires to permeate the talisman until it resonates in harmony with your soul.

Bring your favourite gods or spirits to bless the object and guard your investment.

Additionally, you can apply a basic grounding spell to the talisman when you're possessed of extra energy. It is done by burning sage and sandalwood in a slate disc before placing a candle of white placed on top of the natural stones. Attach the flame to the candle by sitting its direction and firing on it, while the flame moves.

Relax and take deep breaths while you gaze at the flame. Visualize root growth in your legs and arms.

See the roots burrowing deeply into the ground, and sense your connection to the ground and with the cosmic realm. Utilize the roots to release the tiniest of worries and fears and then feel them vanish in the depths of earth. Focus on breathing while you feel the negative energy disappear.

How To Use Roots and Magic Herbs in Spell Work

The rolling of candles into dried roots and herbs will aid in burning the candle more efficiently.

Roast dried herb and roots on slate discs or charcoal.

Use incense

The stronger herbs may be burned directly. Herbs that are flammable, such as rosemary, sage Italian cypress and eucalyptus should be handled with care.

Make use of the roots and plants for tinctures that ensure that their energy lasts for several months at an time.

Chapter 8: Hoodoo Divination

Divination was a privilege restricted to professionals or those who had the talent of predicting that other people's fates. Practitioners who are not practicing would seek the advice of such people and ask for readings for them. When Hoodoo gained more popularity the practitioners realized that they were only able to perform rituals, but had no option to buy crystals, tarot cards or other items.

In the end, they utilized household items as instruments for divination rites. They made use of ordinary cards instead of tarot cards, and used ordinary objects in place of ivory used for the purpose of cleromancy.

Cartomancy

Cartomancy is divination made using an assortment of cards. Gypsies employed regular cards to predict the future. They used the four suits represent the four elements namely the elements of earth, wind and water. Every suit of cards has an order of leadership that represents the individuals and leaders. The Queen and King are represented by their pages. The rest are their subjects that serve their pages.

Card Spreads

This is the term used to describe how cards are dealt, and also what you can expect from the sequences.

Single cards help find quick responses to specific queries.

Three-card spreads can be used to symbolizing the past, predetermined and the future.

Nine-card spreads function similarly as a three-card spread, but with additional data.

Gypsy Spider Web Gypsy Spider Web is made from 21 separate cards that are arranged into three rows with seven cards with more specific details about the past, current, and the future.

The Meaning Behind the Cards

The Suits

Hearts: Hearts are a symbol of the fire element and are associated with the home as well as to issues in relation to feelings.

Diamonds: Diamonds are the symbol of wind, and they are associated with issues that are related to work.

Clubs: Clubs are the representation of the planet and deal with financial and other matters.

Spades: Spades symbolize water and can be associated with obstacles and roads that may result in life-threatening issues.

The Individual Cards

King The King is a wise person with great advice

Queen She is beautiful lady with hair that is light

Jack Jack: Jack is a person younger who has blonde hair

Ten is the symbol of happiness and joy

Nine: Nine is the number that means your dreams and hopes are going to come true

Eight: Eight is a sign that you'll be socially active and get better

Seven: Seven can mean the sham and breaking promises.

Six: Six is a sign of luck and serendipity.

Five: Five represents envious people

Four: Four refers to the change in environment, or perhaps a marriage to be in the near future

Three: Three signifies that you must slow down and stay alert

Two: Two is an unshakeable connection, wealth, and ultimate success

Ace. The Ace symbolizes joy, love, and the beginning of a new chapter

DIAMONDS

King An imposing, but determined and stubborn man, with blonde hair

Queen a flirtatious lady who enjoys gossip

Jack is a younger man with blonde hair, who's often the black sheep in the family.

Ten Ten represents a new context, along with the possibility of success and positive change

Nine Nine is a news source on the financial aspect and your career

The Eight Eight symbolises the onset of marriage maturity, traveling to a cold climate, as well as financial change

Seven Seven represents work-related matters along with surprising presents

Six Six addresses issues related to second marriages

Five Five symbolizes a blissful family life, and a successful career

Four Four represents money, and also unexpected legacy or bequests

Three Three is a legal issue especially in relation to families

Two Two is a symbol of love that's not conventional relationships

Ace Ace represents correspondence related to financial concerns

CLUBS

King King is a loving and kind man sporting dark hair

Queen A beautiful confident and confident lady of older age, with dark locks

Jack A trustworthy younger friend with dark hair.

Ten represents the luck of foreign travel as well as economic news

Nine is a symbol of new relationships in romantic love.

Eight symbolizes relationship and marriage issues

Seven Ways to take care of when it comes to work? Different genders; it also indicates prosperity and riches

Six Reasons to ask for help regarding finances; it also implies that you can succeed in doing business

Five Represents the new friends as well as an happy wedding

Four Means: Bad times are on the way, and you'll be confronted with deceit and betrayal

Three Represents your marriage to an individual who is wealthy or financial support from your spouse

Two Represents lies, backstabbing and two

Ace Provides information on the financial sector as well as health, happiness as well as wisdom

SPADES

King A confident, self-confident man, with black jet hair.

Queen A deceitful and immoral widow with dark hair

Jack is a younger man, with a an unreliable reputation, but who is still unseasoned and well-meaning.

Ten represents bad luck, and fears

Nine Represents all-encompassing misfortune, and even death.

Eight is the number of cancellations as well as disputes within the family as well as at work.

Seven Represents friendships that have been lost

Six represents small victories which result in significant changes

Five is a representation of external influences that can disrupt the household

Four Represents poor health and issues with finances

Three is a symbol of infidelity.

Two Represents difficult decisions regarding partnerships

Ace symbolizes the death of a person, disputes and passions

It is important to remember that some decks have jokers to play their cards. A joker in cartomancy is a new beginning and taking chances.

How to Shuffle Your Deck

There's not a single way to go about the way to shuffle a deck to reveal cartomancy. If you're shuffled quickly, it means that you're trying to find answers in the quickest time possible. A little more time signifies that you're looking for a broad range of literature.

Readers are required to split the deck in multiple piles. People who cut in the shallow end may not trust their advice whereas people who have cut deeper have confidence in the outcomes that the person who reads them will provide.

The most gifted readers are based on a combination of expertise and their the intuition. The story is just the beginning of their journey. If you are consistent and practice, the more result you'll get.

Augury

Augury is a type of divination, which involves the reading of symbols and signs to tell the future. It is believed to go to Ancient Egyptian times, although the formal practice of augury is believed to have been developed in Rome.

The word is taken from Latin auspicium and aupex meaning "looking to birds." It means the earliest people who used this divination practiced the movements of birds in order in order to obtain results.

One of the most potent first steps that you can make in pursuing this type of divination is to let birds appear to you. The presence of wild birds indicates that they are bringing you a message from God's world.

Types of Birds and Their Meaning

Ravens and Crows

Black birds such as ravens and Crows are usually linked with bad or death. luck. It could be due to their coloring. However, any such notions need to be avoided when performing Hoodoo. Actually, the black birds can be a signpost of positive messages. They also bring luck and provide protection.

Hawks

Hawks are a symbol of foresight. They are able to see better than others and indicates that you must become more conscious of the surroundings around you and look at the bigger scene with deliberate consideration and shrewdness.

Owls

Owls are considered to be psychopomps in certain cultures. They are either spirits or animals who are sent down to earth to help guide the soul towards heaven. According to Hoodoo auspicious, owls are believed to indicate that the person who died is likely to be killed. Native Americans even believe that the birds were being sent by spirits of evil to watch over humans.

Hummingbirds

They may appear to be tiny birds however they're strong and stunning they are always beautiful to look at. Hummingbirds' appearance signifies that spirits are transmitting a message of joy and love. Their move is amazing and is nature's way to show you the beauty of harmony.

Doves

Doves have been viewed for centuries as symbols of hope and good intentions. Others, however, view doves as symbolizing death. But, they do not necessarily mean a good symbol.

Observing Birds and Reading Flight Patterns

What number of birds are there and their behavior will help you with how to interpret the messages they convey. One bird usually is signalling to recharge your psychic faculties. They are usually romans as well as multiple birds highlight the power of faith.

Also, you should be aware of whether the birds fly or have acted in a bizarre way. Certain birds exhibit unusual behavior in order to signal physical danger like a hurricane or fire. Or even an earthquake.

Are birds flying toward the South or towards the East? South symbolizes the love of a lifetime, and East is a symbol that is a place of rest or heaven. West can mean two things. It can mean dark or divine blessing and release. North however, on the other hand, refers to performing.

Cleromancy

Cleromancy is an ancient method that enables divination through casting many. Bones have traditionally been used in this method, however it is possible to use all sorts of objects to practice Cleromancy. It could be stones, shells or dice, and even dominos.

Curing Bones

If you're looking to utilize bones for cleromancy make use of turkey or chicken bones. First, boil the water in a pan for 20 mins. Make sure that the flesh has been thoroughly removed prior to taking out the bones and letting them be cool. After that, fill a container with half a gallon of water as well as 1 cup bleach. The bones should be soaked within this solution for one half an hour.

Then, you can make sure that the bones are blessed with Sage smudging, or rub them by rubbing them with oil and then place them within holy salt.

Using The Bones

Yes/No Method

Use a bone to pose a question directly. Place the bone on the altar or table and, if the bone is in a vertical position, there is no answer. If the bone rests horizontally it is a yes.

Scrying

It involves the interpretation of pictures created by the bones. Pick a few bones, and place the bones on a floor from an elevation of about one foot. Focus on the image formed by the bones, and think about what it is trying to convey to you.

Oneiromancy

Oneiromancy is the science of divination using the interpretation of dreams. These are the most popular dreams and their meanings.

Driving

Cars are the symbol for soul. If you imagine driving the car, that means that your life is in transformations. If you're a passenger this could mean you have to be in charge of your choices.

Chapter 9: Hoodoo Spells For Love And Luck

Love spells can be a wonderful option to build relationships by returning lost love. But, if your marriage is in disarray and it is destined to fall apart even the most powerful Hoodoo spells can help it. It is likely that it is possible to cast spells that assist you and your loved one navigate difficult situations within your relationship, particularly when the issue isn't grave.

Create a Safe Space

When casting a love spell be sure you and your loved one are both physically and mentally an safe area. The positive vibes surrounding you helps your relationship to become more open to the spell.

There are gods associated with love you could seek for help, like Aphrodite as well as Cernunnos.

Be sure to pick the right spell Be aware that the spell usually has negative consequences.

Be sure to follow the directions carefully and learn what the consequences could be.

Quick Conciliation Spell

The spell can be used to help two individuals reconnect in the aftermath of a dispute.

There is a need for a paper that has the handwritten text from Psalm 32 along with a candle that is pink and 8 tacks. You will also need an jar of honey as well as a slate and a pin needle.

For the first time begin the spell, you must take a notepad and flip it over inscribe the name of the other person in the space. Pick up a needle or pin and cut the name of that individual into your candle 3 times.

Then, place your candle on a slate piece, and then surround the base with Tacks. Make sure to cover the tacks with honey. It can "sweeten" the pain caused by separation. Light the candle three consecutive days while you recite Psalm 32. Your spell will take effect at the end of the third day.

Honey Jar Spell

This spell can be used to improve relationship that has become dull. If you are looking to revive romantic feelings and love Use this spell.

To do this, you'll require a pencil and paper, as well as a piece of slate, red or pink candles, roots and herbs which you love for example, magnolia or rose petals attraction oil or powder, as well as honey-filled jars.

First, you must note the name of your partner person on the sheet of paper 3 times. After that, you must rotate the piece of paper, and then write your name the exact number of times, so it is a solid block overwriting the name of your companion. Inscribe the block with phrases of love or phrases such as "return to me" or "love me" and do not lift the pen.

Include oils and herbs to the paper along with any other items that are personal to you preference. Add body fluids or even hair pieces to enrich the look. Then, fill the container with roots, plants, and other things related to romantic love.

Put the newspaper in the honey jar, and repeat the following words "This honey is delicious to me, just as (say your name) the name of your companion) is kind and sweet for me."

Take a few drops of honey out of your hands, and perform the same ritual 2 more times. Then, close the jar and place it in a cool, dry place.

Put the candle onto the slate, and then anoint it with honey that you have poured from the container. Lighting the candle, and asking for the assistance of your beloved spirits and gods. Continue this process for 3 days and then your spell will be cast.

Getting Rid of an Unwanted Lover

This spell helps in getting the love of your life or break up with a couple who should not be with each other. To cast this spell, you'll require a rose in red as well as a sheet of paper bearing the name of the person you wish to off or the couple that is involved as well as four nails as well as the is hammer.

Begin by dressing the piece of paper using the oils that help to banish or with herbs for example, sage or garlic. The paper should be folded so it is able to be folded to form the petals of the rose. Find an old tree, and then nail the combination of rose and paper with four nails. Smash the flower to destroy the flower. Return home and not look at the back of your eyes, and your magic is done.

A Spell to Attract New Love

The spell is effective for males and females. It is intended to create love and tenderness. The spell attracts the natural kind of love, and does not make someone love your. To perform this magic it is necessary to have an altar or table and a candle for marriage in white and a rose the bush's thorn.

Make the ritual happen by setting up your altar or table by using objects that are symbolic of your relationship with the person you cherish. They could be items of clothing photographs, memorabilia, or other items. Pick the thorn from the rose bush, and write on the candle with, "Come to me, my heartfelt love" along with your name and the title of the individual you're attracted to. Repeat this 3 times.

Light the candle at the altar, and envision the person moving towards you, with beautiful intentions.

When the candle has burned down to a complete halt, remove the candle's wax puddle as well as all the other things off the altar, and then store them in a safe place.

Luck Spells

This time lets focus on spells that will bring luck and riches. It is crucial to make the proper space the use of wealth and luck spells. Chances will favor you after you cast these spells. However, the spells you cast will be stronger if you spend the time to design the ideal place to use them.

Setting Up Your Altar

It doesn't have to be elaborate in order to function. It can be as easy as having a table within any room of your house. Most important to be aware of is that this altar is only employed for the purpose of magic and spells.

It is possible to personalize your altar and create a symbol of your beliefs. It is possible to decorate it using diverse colored candles or covers that represent your intention when you perform your ritual.

Green is the colour to use in spells that attract fortune and prosperity. Place the altar on cloth in green, or you can use candles that are green for spells for more effectiveness.

Additionally, you can charge your altar with four elements, by putting an sand-filled jar in the north as well as a bowl containing water in the west, and an incense stick on the east, and finally a lit candle of green in the south.

It is also possible to make your altar a place for divine gods and goddesses that are lucky. Ganesh is one example. Ganesh is one of the Indian god who symbolizes success and prosperity. Mahakala is also known as an omen of luck like Ganesh, the Egyptian God Bes.

Good Luck Spell

In order to perform a standard luck-based spell, you'll require three candles in the form of three green ones as well as three pieces of the acorn as well as an incense. To cast the spell you need to place three candles in an arc and then place an acorn in every corner. Incense and candles are lit close to each other and repeat this prayers: "Lady luck and all her companions, I beg to be helped by you. I ask you to grant me the power that a bear has and the luck of rabbits. I call forth the four elements that will bless my efforts. Give me prosperity and health and the best luck to my work. accomplish. Let it be so."

The wax from the candle when it is burned out and wrap it up in green silk. Put it into a fruit bearing tree and the spell has been made.

The Money Spell

Simple money spells can be carried out over the course of 9 days in order to achieve positive results. The spell can be used at every time in the daytime, however, it must be performed in the exact time each time. In order to perform this spell it's best to have candles of white and green as well as any oil that promotes prosperity, like eucalyptus or bergamot and jasmine.

The green candle signifies riches and money, whereas the white candle represents your personal identity. It is possible to write your name on the candle's white to get the most out of it.

The first step is to fill the candle with the appropriate oil, and then place them on the altar, about nine inches from each other. Then, you need to ignite both candles, and then continue to pray:

"Money and wealth are available to me in abundance and abundantly three times 3. I am seeking to be enriched without harming my self. Thanks to your support this will happen. If you have money, I'd like to thank your help three times over."

Following this, move the candles one inch further apart and then extinguish the flames. Repeat the process for 9 days. The ninth day is the time to allow the candles to smolder to the point of completeness before wrapping them in white cloth before place them in the mojo bag.

Spell to Grow Your Business

It is possible to use this spell to help if your business which isn't growing regardless of the effort you strive to increase it. In order to perform this spell, you'll require a large dish with a cup of curd, a quarter cup and a mojo bag with red with fast luck oil almond oil, tiny magnet with seven coins along with one red, green blue, yellow and red candle.

Note the name of your company on one piece of paper. Then put the piece of paper on the plates. The symbol of the sun onto the candles, and then anoint them with oils. Set the curd in the over the table and place seven coins to form the form of an horseshoe. Use the candle in green and set it at the uppermost point of the dish, it's blue towards the left, and the yellow to the right and finally the red in the middle.

The magnet should be placed in the middle of the candle and then light the candle in green.

Ask the gods for prosperity, and beg for the help of these gods. Then, light the yellow candle and then continue to pray. The same is true for blue and red candles.

After the candle has gone out, you can take the candle's remains, including the wax as well as the curd and coins put them in your bag of mojo. Take them along with you every time. It is recommended to renew the spell at least every 6 months, or as often as you believe it is essential. This spell is supposed to work and aid your business grow.

Dream Job Spell

Make use of this spell when you want to alter your job and earn more cash. In order to perform this spell, you'll require a piece of paper and pen as well as peppermint oil, a Silver coin, three cloves garlic and a mojo bag in green.

Make a full detail of the job that you've always wanted on piece of paper. Write down your salary expectations as well as the responsibilities you would like to fulfill. Sprinkle your paper with peppermint oil and put the sheet in the mojo bag.

Put the garlic and silver coin into the bag. Recite the prayer seven times.

"Work and love are inextricably linked. I'm blessed by both. Help me discover my best self as well as let my profession develop."

Lucky Seven's Ritual for Money and Success

This is a great illustration of the relationship Hoodoo makes to numerology. This particular ritual is associated with the number 7 and the way it represents luck and prosperity. In order to make this spell work there are eight single dollars with 7 in each of the Federal Reserve numbers. The number will be displayed within the two-digit number on the note, which indicates the back from which note been issued from. Seven is a reference to Chicago the city, and it'll have a signature in addition.

Also, you will require the crystal of clear quartz as well as one iron pyrite crystal also known as fool's gold. an Aventurine Quartz.

It is best if the charges are paid for in a natural manner over time. This won't happen in the same way if you go to the bank and demanded to see the bills you're looking for.

It is important to be patient during this magic spell. After you've gathered all of the necessary bills to pay, you can begin by presenting one to a friend who is close and explain to them the goals you'd like to accomplish. The more individuals involved in the ceremony and the greater the power of the spell will become.

For the seven remaining dollars, put them on your altar, or put them in the form of a money clip made from silver. Set the crystal as well as other items over the money and let them take charge for up to seven days.

When the members of your group give you appropriate dollar bills, exchange these for those you've got in your initial pile. This can bring fresh enthusiasm into your ritual and with time you'll see greater prosperity and more wealth.

Chapter 10: A Background On Hoodoo

Every traveler must start at some point. The place that was always at the very beginning. Our journey to learning Hoodoo by gaining a better understanding of the roots of it. After that, we'll get to the core of the game.

So, What Is Hoodoo?

Let's begin with the obvious one - what do you think of Hoodoo?

This question must be answered because it is important because a lot of sites and books incorrectly portray Hoodoo through the spread of inaccurate facts.

I've searched on the internet to find the meaning literal of the word. Every time I'm shocked by how many sources don't understand the meaning.

If you tried similar things then you'd end the search in a location far worse than where you started. The search will end in frustration and confusion.

Certain websites don't even mention the meaning of Hoodoo is.

Thank goodness for you. I'm going to make everything easy to follow within this guide.

Here's the information you should know: Hoodoo is the foundation of African American spirituality.

In essence, Hoodoo can be described as the first religious system to be adopted from African Americans. It's a religion of culture that is specific and exclusive for blacks in the Americas.

Perhaps you are asking yourself, "How did this religion get its start?"

It's an interesting answer. Let me bring you back to

A Walk Thru' History To Where It All Began

Hoodoo's origins are traced back to the earliest days of slavery trade across the Atlantic.

We as blacks weren't natives of the Americas.

Our ancestors suffered being taken from their motherland (Africa) and then sold off as slaves. The inhumane way of treating slaves took place between 15th and 19th century.

The majority of our ancestors come from regions from Central or West Africa. A few notable tribes who fell the victim of this illegal act were:

Kongo

Igbo

Akan

Mande

Yoruba

Fon

Ewe

Fulbe

The diverse ethnic communities did not speak the same language, but they had some things they shared.

The first is that they both come from Africa and thus were both black-skinned.

Second, colonialists separated family members from them and then sold them as slaves for work on Western plantations. So, everyone were subject to the emotional and physical the suffocation of being oppressed.

They realized that they had to find a way of rebellion against the oppression of slavery. They also had to bear the immense difficulties that came with slavery, they needed to develop methods of keeping their sense of sanity.

What is the best way to address the two urgent needs?

A type of religion that is cultural in nature. It was true that faith proved as the solution for their numerous problems.

Psychologists have known for a long time that individuals have the ability to conquer difficulties of life, withstand or even overcome the odds if they turn towards a god for direction.

In his book how to let go of worrying and begin living Dale Carnegie noted:

"Man doesn't exist for religion. Religion is a necessity to serve the needs of man."

The wisdom of this is what prompted our forefathers to develop the art of Hoodoo.

Why Was It Practiced?

In addition to religion, our forefathers were adept at Hoodoo with different motives. Let's look into what a few the reasons were.

Battling Diseases

In another section, Hoodoo involves using herbs.

One reason that the herbs were incorporated into Hoodoo practices is because Africans were long aware that they had medicinal properties.

Modern medicine was never practiced in Africa. Instead, healers relied on their understanding of the medicinal properties of plants for the treatment of members of their group.

If they were taken prisoner and sold to slavery Some of these pharmacists and healers used their knowledge of herbs to treat sick Africans who were held in captivity.

It could be an unexpected surprise for you to discover that white slaves could at times rely on the wisdom of Africans in order to fight their ailments and other ailments.

As an example, Onesimus, who Cotton Mather had imprisoned and was released as his knowledge of medicine became essential in the elimination of the smallpox epidemic that devastated the entire colony from Boston, Massachusetts.

Counseling

Hoodoo was also useful in offering advice for African Americans who felt they required some kind of help.

With the stress and strains in captivity, it's obvious why mental health issues could occur among the slaves. This would require counselors as well as psychologists.

As I've argued that white psychologists weren't available for enslaved African Americans.

Thus, slaves had only one option: rely upon themselves for this kind of aid. Therefore, counsellors who were of black from the past would turn to Hoodoo to provide advice regarding how they could assist those in need who sought their assistance.

Resistance

Though African slaves worked in white plantations despite their own will It is important to know that slaves often were able to defend themselves using a variety of methods.

They never surrendered to the oppression. Our ancestors instead battled against the white captors with diverse methods. A unique method of resistance which relied upon Hoodoo was using the use of herbs to poison enslavers.

A lot of slaves held advantage in their understanding of herbs, and were able to use this knowledge to combat oppression poisoning whites as a way to liberate them.

Doctors also make use of plants to invoke spirits who are believed to attack white families and cause suffering.

Preservation Of Cultural Identity

The slave trade between the two continents lasted for decades, and the slaves were getting exposed to American cultures that were quite different from the culture they'd experienced all the time.

This change put their people in danger losing their identity in the land of slavery. Their grandchildren and children could be influenced by the practices of Western society. That is, they'd become Americanized.

Thus, Hoodoo served as the one and only method that communities enslaved by slavery were able to use to connect in their traditional heritage. Hoodoo was the only means they would be able to remain faithful to the traditions of their ancestral homeland.

Is Voodoo and Hoodoo Similar?

Since a couple of years I've had clients come to me seeking advice about Voodoo questions. Every time I've had to be sure to explain the fact that what I do is Hoodoo and not Voodoo.

A lot often time the people aren't aware of what's going on. There are a lot of people consider Hoodoo as well as Voodoo as two different things.

You might make the same error.

This is why I've gone to the time to outline what the differences are between them in this book.

The first thing to note is that Hoodoo and Voodoo aren't the same thing.

The two may sound alike however they're different things.

What's the difference?

It is important to understand the fact that Voodoo is a religion of the culture which originated in Haiti. Thus, although Hoodoo is often associated to African Americans, Voodoo is frequently linked to Haitians.

The name of the practice comes from Vodou meaning "spirit" (or "deity" within the Fon language.

A further distinction is the fact that Voodoo originated from a mixture of African culture and Roman Catholicism prevalent in Haiti with the French settlers in the slave trade across the Atlantic.

You may have read that African slaves ultimately overthrew French rule which colonized Haiti at the end of the 1700s in pursuit of the freedom they had always wanted.

As the revolution swept over control of the nation, a lot of Voodooists as well as their former masters left the country. They sought refuge in Louisiana's port Louisiana located in New Orleans, which was controlled by the Spanish administration.

The Haitian immigrants carried with them practices associated with Voodoo. Over time it was apparent that the ritual of Voodoo was to become associated with the Louisiana region that is New Orleans.

However, the tradition of Voodoo is active and present in Haiti the country from which it was born. The ruling and political classes in the area still admire the practice.

So, now you've accumulated an understanding of Hoodoo information now, it's time for us to begin exploring the basic principles of the practice. This will be the subject in the following chapter.

While you wait In the meantime, here's a short reflective exercise for your own reflection.

Reflection exercise

Now I'd like to track your genealogy. Discover a bit about your origins. Ask your immediate relatives on those prior generations and those who preceded your grandparents, great grandparents and on.

But it's not just this. Find what their position was regarding the subject of Hoodoo. Are they all a adherent or practitioner? It's not easy However, you can discover as much information as you are able to.

Once you have gathered as many details as you are able to write down what you have learned on the next page in your journal.

And then, join me in another chapter.

Chapter 11: The Foundations Of Hoodoo

Before we get into the details of learning Hoodoo it is important to be able to comprehend the fundamentals as thoroughly as we can. Knowing these fundamentals is essential in your ability to perform efficient spells that accomplish your desired goal.

It's like learning to drive on a car. If you're new to the sport and want to learn, don't jump into your car and start trying to jam the throttle and experimenting using each of the controls. It's an invitation to catastrophe. It is better to have your instructor is the first to ensure that you know what each component of the vehicle works. And then, only after that will he begin giving your driving lessons.

What are the fundamental components of Hoodoo you need to be able to master? These include:

The spirits of our ancestors

The lineage of your blood or ancestral ancestry is extremely important when it comes to the art of Hoodoo.

Any knowledgeable Hoodoo practitioner who is worth your time will explain Blood magic is considered to be one of the most powerful forms of magic.

What is the reason for this? Since it is directly derived the people that came prior to you, the ones prior to them as well, and so on.

In order to illustrate what I'm speaking about, I'd like to draw your attention to one of the most fundamental principles of Hoodoo. There is a universal belief that you're always the manifestation of the ways and actions of your ancestral ancestors.

The same observation is true regardless of whether their actions are good or bad.

I've met a guy in my area who regularly encounters trouble almost every time.

There is a reason why the person who is always in this position isn't lucky. Strangely, bad things seem to be a sign of his character.

In one instance I got a call from him telling me that he'd fractured his arm.

"You injured your arm? What caused it?"

"I was taking the garbage bags, I got sloppy on some liquid which had spilled over the road and was thrown off the pavement and fell. I'm in great discomfort." He was crying. I felt sorry for his pain.

Later, just a few days after being released from the hospital, a car was able to hit his vehicle from behind, while along the highway.

In the present, having accidents every occasionally is fine. This man, however, had two incidents within the space of just a few days.

He was rushed into the hospital for stitches repaired.

You may have met someone such like this one in your daily life.

Whatever they do, or how they turn out the person is able to attract bad luck.

If you take a careful examine this person's family tree and family tree, you'll likely gain some clues about what might be taking place.

Maybe the ancestral ancestors were bad individuals. Perhaps they hurt others in a deliberate way. Perhaps someone of their victims decided to curse their family lineage.

Maybe you've encountered one who appears to be having the most easy time with life. Positive things are always happening for this individual. Then they're not even able to be trying hard.

There is a good chance that the person's parents were decent people who performed good deeds and were adored by a lot of people.

That is the power of the ancestral spirits.

If you contact your family members, you could gain guidance regarding how you can approach things in your own day-to-day life.

Your family's ancestors are blessed with the benefits of knowledge. They've also committed errors in the past. This is why they are able to see the things you don't normally be able to see. Getting their advice will stop your from making costly errors in your life, and repeating your mistakes in the future.

One thing to note regarding the old magic is that it's effectiveness is rarely ever sufficient without first being acknowledged.

What do you need to do for it?

We'll learn more in the later chapters, there's ways of pleasing your ancestors.

However, here's a simple suggestion to be aware of.

There is an area for them in your home. Maybe you can think of the possibility of a table and a chair where you think they'll place their feet. It is possible to reserve some beverages, such as water or food items, or even alcoholic drinks to drink frequently.

Root Magic

Hoodoo may also be known as RootWork.

This name is a result it was the common usage of herbs and roots to create spells and awe-inspiring mystical effects in Hoodoo the Hoodoo culture.

The usage of roots has a the context of a good reason, naturally. The fact is, prior to the time that humans were ever able to comprehend technology and science, as currently the only thing we had was the natural world.

Nature never fails to please.

Nature was able to meet our all needs. It did not matter if that needs were spiritual, emotional or physical. Nature was able to meet this desire.

It was then that we realized that plants can resolve problems that seemed more obscure.

In my previous chapter, I explained how a Hoodoo doctor was able to fight an outbreak of smallpox.

However, that is only one of the many benefits of roots and plants within Hoodoo lifestyle.

As an example, you could utilize some of the roots to make spells to attract the love of your life. There are also several spells to cast fidelity on your loved one.

We'll explore RootWork more in depth in the coming chapters However, it is important to understand that root systems are an essential part of Hoodoo which you shouldn't ignore.

Spirits Of The Earth

One of the most important, exciting elements of Hoodoo is earth like soil.

Earth generally has magical potential due to the energy that flows through it.

If you splash a small amount of water onto a garden's soil, it is quick to absorb it similar to the way sponges soak up water.

The ground is able to absorb the energy from the surrounding in a similar method.

You can also utilize the energy that is stored in the earth for a many purposes.

In other words, the earth that is on the productive land has the entire energy required for farmland efficiency.

If I were conducting a spell to improve the efficiency of my farm the soil that is derived from a successful neighbor's farm is one of the primary elements.

Let's take a look at this in a different method.

If I'm looking for a magic spell which will bring wealth I'd suggest the use of earth that is close to the bank.

Do you understand the notion?

If you are considering casting any spell, use, check whether you are able to use earth with a specific type of energy that makes it work.

The earth can utilized for a different important purpose: the ability to ground spells.

The magic that is connected to roots, ancestral spirits, or even anything else can be, without doubt highly effective. Whatever its power however, it isn't always stable.

This instability could result in all kinds of unanticipated problems.

Imagine the electric pole. It is erected by the power company for the purpose of transporting electricity cables. However, for it to perform its job it must be securely grounded in soil. If it's not grounded, it's likely to slide and cause a variety of chaos.

Magic is the same. It will require a method of anchoring it and then directing it to perform the type of thing you want it to perform.

It is possible to, for instance casting a wealth spell by using the earth that surrounds an area for banking, but If a criminal deposits the money in that area it could result in having misfortune with the individual too.

However, if you are using ground that is sourced from a particular location such as a church, you could ground your spell to counteract the evil that is that are associated with the magic.

Are you able to relate to the way it is done?

Graveyards

Then we come to an Hoodoo component that's truly controversial: graveyard spirits.

It is essential to be cautious when dealing in graveyard spirits. New Hoodoo practitioners are prone to fall and cause themselves in a lot of problems. I'd advise against doing work using graveyard spirits, at the very least, at first.

The art of dealing with the spirits of graveyards is typically recommended for older and more skilled professionals who have worked with spirits for a long time.

Why?

Graveyard spirits typically aren't tolerant of disruptive disturbances. They prefer to remain calm and unaffected. You need a great deal of talent in order to convince them to join forces and collaborate together.

Another risk of working with the spirits of graveyards is that you could trip over yourself, and commit the error of using the spirit of your deceased loved ones who were unlucky, and thus attracting your attention all kinds of negative luck and devil.

Make sure you're working with the right person and act in a manner that is respectful of them.

However, working with the spirits of graveyards is like dealing with the earth spirit, in the sense that, in both instances it is a matter of relying on the power of soil for the power to perform.

What is the purpose. What's the meaning of the graveyard?

In general, it is utilized as a marker for transitional times This means that you could make use of it to mark new beginnings or end points in your life.

It's possible that you've endured the pain of poor luck in your relationships. It's time to stop the cycle and begin afresh. Grave magic could be a key element in resolving your dilemma.

In conclusion, let me declare that the work of working with graveyard spirits is the responsibility of specialists. Consider consulting an expert who has the experience of successfully working with graveyard spirits to help in this kind of magical activity.

Crossroads

If you've been curious about Hoodoo writing for a while it is possible that you've seen or heard about the famous phenomenon crossroads, and thought "what does it mean really?"

It's great that you've asked:

Similar to the magic of graveyards, the crossing of the road can be the catalyst for new beginnings in one's life.

The main difference is that the magic of crossroads does not have anything to do with ending anything.

Because of this, crossing paths can open doors to possibilities in the world of the world of.

It's possible that you've worked over the years trying to find work with minimal or no potential. There's a chance to make a magic spell to set you on a journey that can bring you prosperity in the form of money and employment opportunities.

Purification and Cleansing

A lot of new Hoodoo students make the mistake of engaging in spells and spells, but not performing purification or cleansing rituals. Do not make similar mistakes.

Similar to how cleansing and purification ceremonies are essential in many other religions, such as Christianity, Hoodoo is no one-off. People who do not take this vital step tend to be frustrated when their attempts at performing magic rarely produce result.

Why is this happening? What makes purification and cleansing essential for Hoodoo?

The reason isn't related to physical hygiene that makes you unworthy of the spirit.

In reality, this is due to the fact that you find yourself emotionally and spiritually locked in ways that you don't even know or even contemplate.

If this is the scenario, you'll be in a position to not manifest the dreams and desires you are seeking the for the most important things in your life.

Cleansing and purification rituals can enable you to be for receiving the guidance and blessings that Spirits send to you.

You will discover later the process of purification and cleansing is not difficult. The simple practice of throwing certain parts or medicinal herbs onto your body generally will accomplish the task.

The effect is usually felt almost instantly. If you're paying attention you will be able to notice the change that occurs in you when it happens.

The Bible

I put this part in the last time because I wanted to highlight an important fact.

People mistakenly think the term "hoodoo" Hoodoo practiced one has no faith in God.

The media and film depict and frequently depict and often Hoodoo with evil and sorcery. They portray Hoodoo as well as other religions, like Voodoo with regard to devil worshipping. This is a deliberate attempt to depict people who follow Hoodoo as being out of need for a place in the church or likely even in the society.

This is a mistake. I've had the pleasure of meeting many Hoodoo experts who are more committed church supporters than any other I've had the pleasure of meeting. It is my opinion that those who think this way don't know about the past of Hoodoo.

The belief in God is an integral aspect of Hoodoo in such a way it is said that Bible is among Hoodoo's primary elements.

Black people within The States very much identify with the biblical story of Israelites that Moses released from captivity. The few components in Hoodoo are as reverent to the Bible. It is considered to be the greatest magic book for Hoodoo.

Of particular importance is The Book of Psalms. It's such a potent grimoire that thousands of magic techniques have been pulled out of it by highly skilled Hoodoo practitioners.

We'll look at the spells in subsequent chapters.

How to Make Your OilHere's a thing you should to learn about the subject of oils and powders. Although it's generally acceptable to buy the products from a third party like the Hoodoo professional - absolute joy and power comes by learning how to prepare the ingredients yourself.

If you opt for this option then you'll have greater control over the items you prepare in any particular moment. Additionally, you will have a range of possibilities of what to include, and what should not include.

It isn't difficult to imagine how hard it is to locate true love, particularly in the current climate. That's why I've included a straightforward procedure to help in the preparation of your Hoodoo oil, which you could use to build yourself an attraction to love. Make use of this oil to increase the chances of falling in love which appear within your life.

Exercise: Preparing Love Drawing Oil

Before I begin we need to draw an issue. Making magical oils requires using a carrier oil which is neutral.

There are two kinds of coconut oil that I like more than the other - coconut oil and olive oil.

The great thing about this type of oil (and coconut oil, in particular) is that they rapidly modify their structure to suit what is contained in the ingredients that are contained within them.

In other words, I could include powerful herbs the resulting oil will be altered and more dense. In the same time I can use a gentle substance, and anticipate the oil to take on an appearance of softness.

These oils are however in no way the only option that are available. There are other almond and grapeseed oils in this regard as well:

What You'll Need

Patchouli - For enhancing passion

The rose petals are a beautiful symbol of affection

The rind of the orange (dried)

Jasmine oil

Steps

1. The first step is to find a clear glass bottle, and add the coconut oil or olive oil.

2. Then, you add the previous ingredients, one at a to mix them together.

3. Allow the mixture to sit throughout the day. After that, make use of filters to remove

the liquid. Repeat this procedure over three days. While you're at making sure that there are there are no leaves within the liquid.

4. Keep shaking the liquid each day for a maximum of 7 days. When this time is up the oil will be all set to be used.

Every throughout the day, apply a little of this oil on any part of your body like your hands or face. It will serve as a lucky charm that draws the attention of people and lovers you might be attracted to frequently.

This is the way you can typically make a straightforward form of Hoodoo oil. Different processes can involve various elements, however they all follow the same procedure. You now know the steps to make your first oil, maybe you're asking:

What Is The Best Way To Store Hoodoo Oil?

Let's address that question quickly using the following guidelines to follow while storing Hoodoo oils:

Utilize a dark glass vial or bottle.

If you are planning to use clear bottles or vials make sure you keep them in a dark box or container.

Make sure the bottles are kept at a temperature that is cool and away from pet and children.

If you're familiar with oils, why not learn some things about candles? This will be the subject on the next chapter.

However, before we forget we should do a small workout, right?

Reflection Exercise

Discuss how the process of making the oil felt to you. Recall your experiences when you were searching for components. What was your experience? Did you find it exciting? Exciting? Boring? Easy?

How did you feel following the use of the oil. Was your body reacting differently? How did people react toward you? Was it more welcoming? Have your relationships changed in a positive way? Do you have a couple of potential partners.

Chapter 12: Candle Magic

Let's discuss another important aspect of Hoodoo magic: candles.

Through the years I've discovered that many experienced Hoodoo practitioners are without candles. However, I've noticed that most beginners overlook how important candles are in casting spells.

Similar to the majority of people who have just discovered Hoodoo You're likely to be wondering, "what about candles makes these candles so distinctive to this particular spirituality?"

The Oneness Of Mind

I'm sure you remember me speaking previously about how important concentration is crucial to getting results in the Hoodoo spells.

Through years of training I've discovered that a mind with no focus will be unable to realize its goals. This kind of mind can be compared to an uncontrolled boat that is pushed across a multitude of directions, limiting its ability.

But nothing, in fact, will stop an mind with clarity of intention and thought.

I've discovered that a lot of individuals don't know the components employed for Hoodoo magic (such as earth, herbs oil, and so on.) are not just ghosts that are dormant and waiting for someone to come in and take them over. It takes strong, well-trained brain to get them to be cooperative.

Experience have taught me that distracted minds are among the major reasons for why most spells cast do not work or finish with unexpected results.

Due to the conflicting desires within their heads, many individuals fail to reach an understanding of those who are the spirits of the elements that are used for the spells they're trying to use.

You could, for instance, try casting an oath to attract your lover to you. Your mind could be occupied by the thoughts of revenge and emotions. Your inability to connect your goals and the forces that are in front of you could result in your failing to fulfill the magic.

There are a handful of people in our society actually have the capacity and ability to be able to focus their mind at a specific subject. It's been my experience that these people aren't the norm. It is true that this ability requires time and time to develop and develop in a way that's practical.

The majority of us lack the same level of mental discipline. In fact, fewer are able to commit the time needed to develop this ability easily. There are spells that may require immediate attention.

Then, what should we do?

It is essential to have things that assist us with focusing our mind and determination. This is why candles can be found They make the task of focussing our thoughts much easier, so we can achieve whatever we desire.

The Power Of The Candle Flame

The magic of candles lies in the light they produce.

A candle's flame is able to draw your attention and hold your attention. The flame emits a certain sort of glow which can draw you closer to the spiritual side of you.

The light of this is one of the primary reasons that meditation techniques encourage the use of candles. The light of a candle can soothe the most agitated minds.

If you are glued to the flame of a candle and you begin to ignore the other distractions that surround the flame. In time, you realize that your mind's focus does not shift across the spectrum of your thoughts towards another, but instead is focused upon a particular thought an object, feeling, or thought.

Types Of Candles and The Purposes They Serve

Hoodoo lets you use various candles. Today technology has made it possible to make candles that have different shades of color that weren't available earlier. Our forefathers could have access to some of the fundamental shades. These are those colors that we'll be discussing in the present:

Black Candles

I understand what you're thinking. It is likely that you have assumed that black is associated with the evil. So, it is likely that candles with black color have an important place in spells that include dark or evil magic. It's funny how many folks would think the same.

Although the notion appears to make a lot number of sense, fact is that the black candles are used for much more noble reasons. A good example is protecting and protection.

If you are planning casting a spell which shields you from the effects of negative energies This candle will surely prove useful.

Also, it can come in handy if you need to cast a spell which requires you to dominate someone else's.

As an example, say there's a stalker who's making you feel uncomfortable. If you're so inclined, the black candle could aid in eliminating this person from your existence.

Red Candles

It's true that the color red represents affection. In fact it is a candle that has an important spot in spells that deal with issues of love, passion and attraction.

Red candles can help in different situations. As an example it can be deeply emotional, and may help for spells involving the concept of revenge.

White Candles

White is the color which is most commonly used. In the majority instances, it's the candle you'll use.

We've been taught by society to think of white as pure tranquility, peace and harmony. This is the reason it is likely that you will want to light the candle in which peace of mind are essential.

Green Candles

If you think about green as a color What images spring to the forefront?

For me, I see vegetation. It could be the same for you.

This is probably the reason our forefathers were able to connect this particular candle with growth, fertility and wealth.

But there's another thing connected with candles that are green and that's money. It's the type found on the common dollar bill. There was the time that the color green was everywhere on the bill. This is probably why our ancestors chose to link this particular candle with the success of a business.

If you are planning to perform a ritual which involves blessing your own or another person the candle you choose to use should be on your list of items to purchase.

Blue Candles

Blue candles are beneficial for those who want to boost healthy mental wellbeing because the blue hue often evokes an optimistic spirit like the angel.

If I come at home tense, stressed and anxious I will always soak in warm baths or light the blue candle and then meditate in my room for about 30 minutes.

It is my experience that this easy routine is capable of helping me relax and soothe my spirit. In these nights, I sleep as an infant baby I awake the next day in a state of mind that is like being a brand new person.

Yellow Candles

Candles that are yellow can be exciting due to their capacity to bring out a cheerful spirit.

This color of yellow has this amazing capability to eliminate blues and boost your mood.

If you're skeptical start your day and go out in the morning to the beach when the sun just beginning to rise. It will instantly give you an uplifting and warm feeling within you. In a flash, you'll realize that you've earned it all in the end.

It's the same at night in the evening when the sun is getting ready to go down. If you're around watching the radiance creates in the sun, you'll understand the concept.

This is one reason why this kind of candle is just so wonderful for those who are experiencing some down time within your life, and you're feeling slightly sad. This candle is a great mood booster.

Silver Candles

One of the most common uses for silver candles is to mimic moonlight's power.

It is possible to perform Hoodoo spells that require channelling the energies that the moon has. Problem is that the moon doesn't always appear visible in the sky other than during certain times during the year or month.

If you're in desperate require of performing an emergency ritual in between moon cycles, you'll be at an extreme advantage. There is a way to work it with a silver candle to replace the moon's position in the sky, and then you're ready to start.

The Art Of Interpreting Candle Signals

As we wrap up our candle-related discussion, let's discuss how to discern the messages that they convey. This skill is necessary if hope to perform effective spells in the near future using candles.

The lessons I have learned from experience are that the very first factor you must understand is that reading candles is an art of the highest level which could take all of a book. Since this book is written for newbies, let's quickly go over the essentials you'll require to learn in order to make the most of candles in your work.

Three things to look out for are:

The color of the flame

The movement of the flame

The intensity of the flame

Let's look at each of these factors:

The Flame Color

The flame of candles will come in diverse colors that range between blue and red. Additionally, you'll see shades of orange and yellow within.

If you notice red hue in a flame, it's an indication that a powerful Spirit or entity is in the area. Red color is an indication to take caution.

When you notice an emerald flame that is blue is a sign of that it is the home of a kind spirit, such as that of an angel, or perhaps a good-hearted ancestral relative.

The orange or yellow flame indicates that you are in the presence of active, positive energy which you can utilize for all goals.

The Brightness Of The Flame

If you're looking at the flame moving at a slower pace it means there is a lack of energies around the spell. The low power indicates that you might be required to boost the power of the spell in order to achieve maximum effect.

If your flame appears to be burning unevenly and violently This could be a sign that the spell is not properly base.

You can tell that things are good when you can see an flame burning consistently and evenly.

The Direction Of The Flame

The direction of the flame is also an indication. But, prior to making any measurements, make sure you're in a completely closed area, away from the winds.

The direction of a flame is towards the east is usually a sign that you're in good health ready for the magic.

If the flame is facing the west, it's usually an indication of the emotional intensity in the area of the power.

If you see a fire that is always pointed towards the north, be aware that the energy of your body has become a key element to the period of.

If your flame is pointing towards the south, recognize that your physical power comes from your intention or willpower which makes it even more potent.

If you're comfortable to candles, we'll talk about a new method for making lasting Hoodoo magic with your name in the following chapter.

Again, here's one of the exercises for your enjoyment.

Reflection Exercise:

At this point, your task is to contemplate lighting a candle. Choose a pleasant color, like white, blue or green. you can light it.

Make sure you're at a comfortable place with no interruptions.

As you are able to do this, using your current understanding of candles, carefully look at the flame. Pay attention to the colors and movements. What does it mean? Record what comes to the mind.

After that, you should meditate on the light of the candle. Clear your mind of all other thoughts. You should be focusing on nothing other than the flame of the candle.

When five minutes are up Note down the difference you are feeling. Do you think this is something you'd be willing to do again?

Chapter 13: Mojo Bags

Before proceeding with our Hoodoo conversation more in depth, I'd want to draw attention to some fundamental flaws in traditional spells.

It is true that any time you perform an omen, be it to protect yourself, love or luck, or something other than that, it is important to understand that the power of your spell diminishes with time. After a while, the spell is no longer as powerful in the same way as it did shortly after you cast it.

In order to ensure that you continue benefitting from an omen and continue to see the magic working You will have to perform a variety of castings in the near future that is, as you could imagine, can be too much work for the new Hoodoo users. Take a look.

In essence, when you're dealing with up to three different instances running at any period, it is possible to check on these a couple of times per week. It can become boring.

In this light, you're probably asking yourself, "what can I do to simplify my Hoodoo work better and more efficient?" Could you, say, for example, create an application that operates in autopilot? Yes, you can. That's why Mojo bags are available.

This chapter will assist you to know the meaning behind what Mojo bags are, and the best way to utilize to benefit from your Hoodoo exercise.

Let's get started"

What Are Mojo Bags and How Do They Work?

There are a myriad of definitions to the word Mojo bag and people have different interpretations of them.

To ensure simplicity, clarity as well as to ensure that we're in the same boat as the discussion goes on Here's the information you'll need to be aware of:

Mojo bags come prepackaged with spells you can customize to accomplish specific goals that you will need in the course of time.

Let's break down the definition so that you can have an improved knowledge of Mojo bags and their main usage for Hoodoo.

First, Mojo bags contain packaged spells. They're focused on the magic of. One of the things I've noticed is that you are able to pack the magic in an approach that permits users to draw on the magic at any time.

The second reason is that the magic contained in Mojo bags is very specific. This means that you must make several Mojo bags to carry out any magic you plan to use. As an example, you could carry a bag to protect protection, love, money or luck etc.

In the end, you'll be able to create Mojo bags that can sustain you in the long term. This is the reason why Mojo bags an integral component of Hoodoo exercise at all.

Think for a second that you're about to embark on an extended trip. It is likely that, on your journey, you'll require food and water.

There are two options for this dilemma. The first is to eat at restaurants along your route and purchase drinks and food each time you are thirsty. This is similar as performing spells every time you believe you'll need one.

In the second, you may choose to take your food items and drinks from home into your car. So, you won't need to make a stop every time to purchase a meal or buy food, as you'll always have it available when you require it.

In truth, I'd rather the other option as it's more of an easy decision. Take a look

How confident can you be in the absence of conveniently situated restaurants and stores on the road? Do you have any control regarding the time the eateries you believe to be on your road trip are in operation? It's not possible! What about the price? Would it benefit both the business owner or proprietor of the premises? Does the food you are served even match your personal preferences?

I'm not sure about you I don't know about you, but for me they sound like lots of unanswered questions, which makes this second alternative more sensible as opposed to the first.

Mojo bags operate in the exact identical way, specifically when casting spells that will last for longer time. If, for instance, you cast a spell to protect yourself and its effectiveness decreases, it's time to recast the spell and you will have to cast each time.

Similar to the sustenance problem that I've discussed in the previous paragraph, the best for a more effective solution is to make your security Mojo bag. The bag keeps your spell in motion, as well as keeping it will keep you protected at all times for as long as you feed it with the vital energy that it requires regularly.

Are you able to see what I'm talking about?

There are two additional uses for Mojo bags that you need to be aware of:

1: Powering Long-Term Spells

Mojo bags are able to provide an extra source of energy the spell requires to sustain it, and allow the effects of a spell to be manifested into your current life. So the Mojo bag functions as batteries that power the traditional Hoodoo spells.

For instance, if you make a magic spell to increase wealth, the is likely to take some time until its results are realized. In order to prevent the power of your spell from fading before it occurs, use the Mojo bag to help fuel the magic and keep it as bright as is possible and thus powerful.

I had one client who came to me with the claim that the magic spell that I suggested was not working for her.

Following her interview I realized that she didn't understand the fact that love spells usually need time before revealing themselves and she had to perform the ritual regularly to work.

Naturally, she was concerned that she would have a hard time and I was in agreement. Therefore, I suggested we create an Love Mojo bags instead. The only thing she would have to do is consist of applying a small amount of attraction oil onto it each week, in order to ensure it remains effective.

In just six weeks, she contacted me with joy, telling me about the new guy she was in love with which she was feeling very happy about. Our small exercise proved successful in helping her achieve the things she was looking for.

2: To Channel Your Inner Strength

The majority of people do not know this, however within it there is an energy force that unfortunately, usually goes into the darkness untapped. It is possible to harness and utilize this power in a variety of ways within your professional, personal or even your spiritual.

Take for example, the times where you're "out out of sorts"--periods where you're feeling unsure and stressed. During these periods, there's the need to be peaceful and at ease.

For many, the capacity to act lies within you. Hoodoo magic is a great way to get it out. An Mojo bag could be a great help in this time.

After you've become in the know about Mojo bags, the question is how can you create your own?

Focus on learning to accomplish that now:

Training: Preparing a Mojo Bag This Mojo bag can assist you to keep your inner peace regardless of turbulent situations.

The modern world is quite difficult. People are facing greater stress than they have ever faced ever before. As the Hoodoo spiritualist, it is impossible to be without an Mojo bag that helps you stay grounded and focused on your spells that you use to bring about positive changes in your lifestyle. This bag is an essential resource.

What You'll Need

The following are the essential items that you'll need to complete this Mojo bag workout:

The seeds of chamomile

Lapis lazuli stone

A seashell

A flannel bag (indigo blue)

Like you may have noticed it isn't my intention to pick one of these objects randomly. All of them have been picked to accomplish a particular reason, and I'll be able to explain in order to provide you with an understanding of the functioning of the ingredients accomplish and the way they operate in conjunction.

Chamomile is well-known throughout the world for its calming properties. As an example, many people are aware that making the chamomile tea following a tiring work day can feel calming and calm, especially following bath or shower.

Hoodoo practitioners have utilized Lapis lazuli stones as a symbol of peace and harmony, which are a major part of the Mojo bag.

Seashells are a popular choice due to their ability to mimic the sounds of the ocean. If you've taken a bite of a shell and put it inside your ear, then you'll know the meaning behind my claim that seashells create the impression of being on a tranquil beach.

In the end, the flannel bags is packed with the vital components that give the Mojo bag its strength. Indigo is a color that has been carefully selected. It symbolizes peace within. It can be soothing on the soul.

Steps

1. Like you would imagine, the initial step is to arrange all the elements above inside the flannel bag. Once you have done that close the bag to ensure the contents are kept within.

2. The next thing to do is to infuse bags with intentions that decades of daily Hoodoo practices have shown me is probably one of the most crucial aspects in an Mojo bag. The process of incorporating your intention to the bag is fairly easy. Simply take the bag with your hands and say these words in a sincere, heartfelt way:

"I am at the moment to give the power of peace to this bag. Each time the bag comes into contact with me I'll feel instantly at peace and feel a sense peace, inner calm and serenity.

When faced with difficult situations I'll be able to keep a calm and calm mindset.

An unwinding mind is exactly what I want This is why I have activated this bag immediately from now onwards."

3. The last stage is breathing into the bag, ensuring that it absorbs your spirit and is a reflection of your personal signature that is the most important aspect of the entire process.

When you've completed these steps After completing the above steps, you'll be able to take possession of your very individual Mojo bag. All you'll need to remember from now to the present, just as if you were on cue is to massage this bag with oil that has been anointed so that the energy in it is not lost and remains effective.

In case I've never previously mentioned it, or you're confused about how to make it, creating an oil that is anointed is easy. The only thing you need to do is mix the mixture that contains Frankincense along with Myrrh (35 drops of each) along with a carrier oil like

Extra Virgin Olive Oil, and then you're good to go.

Then you'll are able to make an easy but effective Mojo bag. This means that we are able to go on to the next aspect you must learn about Hoodoo prayer: the power of prayers!

You've heard that drill. Sure, it's an workout.

Reflection Exercise

Just made your Mojo bag, which is made to encourage inner calm and tranquility.

You should observe your daily life for one week. If and time you are anxious, stressed or stressed, imagine you have a Mojo bag. Note how differently you feel. Do you feel more calm, and more comfortable? Note down the results of your experience.

Do you think that you will use this bag more frequently? Note your comments on this in the same way.

Chapter 14: Hoodoo Prayers

Before we discuss spells, let's look into prayers for a while and learn the role they play in on-hand Hoodoo practice--conversely, Hoodoo prayers will form a very key part of the practice.

Similar to all religions, prayer are a fundamental element of Hoodoo. They may be performed on their own or in conjunction with the spell.

The prayers in Hoodoo are available in three different forms:

i. The Catholic Prayers

ii. Novenas

iii. The Psalms

Let's look at each one.

The Catholic Prayers

In my previous discussions, there is an evident Christianity component in Hoodoo. Christianity is a part of Hoodoo since, while slaves the missionaries introduced our forefathers to Christianity and they got deeply inseparable from it.

Hoodoo has been around for years because it has been incorporated into Christianity which has granted the credibility and recognition it required to be successful within European as well as American culture.

One way by which Hoodoo blends Christianity is through the prayer we offer to those of the Roman Catholic Church.

Then, I'll reveal the prayers of the Catholic Church which Hoodoo users regularly sing. It is important to note that I did not make these prayer chants personally; I do not own them, and they're freely available to the public. So, there's not a need to reproduce these prayers in the book. A simple Google search will bring the pages whenever you want to refer these.

This includes:

The Apostle's Creed

Hail Mary

Home Blessing

The Lord's Prayer

Prayers for home and family

Invocation to the Seven African Powers

Prayer to St. Joseph for Protection

Novenas

They are distinct types of prayers that are unique to. They are unique due to their requirement that you be chanting them before an unbreakable glass casing that holds seven candles that are each designed to last throughout seven consecutive days.

If and time you would like to offer prayers, sit at the exact candle that symbolizes your intentions as well as the angel who is handling your prayer.

Chapter 15: Breaking Hexes

When you are deeper in your spiritual Hoodoo experience and practices it, you'll discover even new uses for the various chapters within the Bible of Psalms.

You might be surprised to learn that prior to getting married to the lover of my life I would get up every morning and go through a passage of Psalms 111. In the morning, I would meditate upon what I done before starting my morning's tasks.

I am confident that this easy morning routine has been instrumental in helping get married with a record time.

After you have learned the various prayers, a problem could stand out more within your head more than the others. The question you should ask yourself is:

How Do You Pray Over Items, Especially When Conducting Spells?

It's an excellent query. There are five main strategies you can employ.

In the beginning, place an object by your fingers and put it near your mouth. It is the intention to position it so that your breath touches the item when you speak, infused the item with your personal essence. This is what we call a signature.

Then, you are able to grab an object, then hold it near your heart.

Thirdly, you could place the object in your palms, then cross your arms in an X shape.

Fourth, if you are praying to light candles, wrap the candles between your palms in your prayer hands that you were taught while learning how to pray as when you were a young child.

Five, if it is not large, put your right hand on top of the left and then hold the object over the top.

www.ingramcontent.com/pod-product-compliance
Lightning Source LLC
Chambersburg PA
CBHW071442080526
44587CB00014B/1958